Virtue and Social Enterprise

Geraldine Hall

Virtue and Social Enterprise

Ethical Alternatives to Capitalism

palgrave
macmillan

Geraldine Hall
South Wales, UK

ISBN 978-3-031-14026-6 ISBN 978-3-031-14027-3 (eBook)
https://doi.org/10.1007/978-3-031-14027-3

This Palgrave Macmillan imprint is published by the registered company Springer Nature Switzerland AG
The registered company address is: Gewerbestrasse 11, 6330 Cham, Switzerland

Foreword: Social Enterprise, Social Economy and Social Goods

That 'social enterprises' provide some kind of ethical alternative to capitalism is a commendable and ambitious proposition. 'Capitalism' has long denoted a historical stage of economic progress, but the old hope for socialism as a further stage, in which labour no longer subserves capital but capital subserves humanity, has receded over the past fifty years as the capitalist horizon appears to extend into the indefinite future. Instead of proposing such a systemic, stadial alternative to capitalism, Geraldine Hall here uses the ethics of Alasdair MacIntyre to support John Pearce's proposal that a 'social economy' be constructed out of social enterprises.

Pearce's schematic proposal was most fully and attractively elaborated in *Social Enterprise in Anytown*, published in 2003 following the attempt of Tony Blair and Gordon Brown's 'New Labour' to supersede Britain's old, Labour left and neoliberal New Right with a 'third way' politics. The next year saw the introduction of a new legal form of enterprise, the 'community interest company', opening what has become a large (if usually local) space between traditional cooperatives and charities and, conversely, capitalism's dominant joint-stock limited-liability corporations. This legislative initiative followed the work of numerous academics, led by Paul Q. Hirst, reworking the past ideas of guild socialists and others into proposals for new organizational forms of economic and social governance, constitutive of a newly pluralist (or 'market') socialism or 'associative democracy'. Linking such academic theory to the Labour Party and, from 1997, government were the likes of the Socialist

Philosophy Group, Charter 88, *Samizdat*, *Renewal* and such theoretically inclined members of parliament as Tony Wright, calling for new forms of enterprise, ownership, industrial democracy and small-scale, local economy.

The idea of a social economy had been slow to enter Britain. Having been formed and financed by its trade unions, its Labour Party had been committed to defending unions' ability to bargain collectively with employers free from interference by government or courts. As policy, 'socialism' denoted state ownership. This took the form of the 'public corporation', which recreated private corporations' institutional division of management from owners and of both corporately, from employed labour. The advantage to trade unions of such 'nationalized industries' was that they were redirected from profitability, for the benefit of shareholders, to such goals as full employment and the maintenance of nationally domestic industry, supposedly guaranteed by government and taxpayers, whilst still allowing unions full freedom from the state. Conversely, many tax-paying voters were persuaded that electorally unaccountable union leaders exercised excessive power over Labour politicians. What had been newest about Margaret Thatcher's New Right, Conservative Party government was its commitment to 'free' ownership from the state and the labour market from union power. Its success persuaded such Labour politicians as Blair and Brown to look for 'social', economic alternatives to nationalization and free collective bargaining. Two easy options were to free the Bank of England from government control and to introduce a state-enforced minimum wage, which added to Conservative legislation in weakening unions' social role. Beyond that, Labour's leadership looked for inspirational principles to the likes of Pearce, Wright and Hirst.

On the continent, ideas of market socialism and social economy had already been around for some time. Tito's Yugoslavia demonstrated its independence from the Soviet, statist model socialism by legislating for workers' self-management, whilst Franco's Spain permitted the politically oppressed Basques of Mondragon the economic freedom to establish their own workers' cooperatives. The latter experiment was justified in terms not of socialism but of 'Catholic social teaching', which in Catholic Portugal warranted the persistence of a 'corporate state' of the kind that had been terminated in Italy along with fascism. In between communist Yugoslavia and Catholic Iberia, Cold War conditions favoured Catholics' Christian Democratic parties competing with Social Democratic parties over the idea of a humane, social economy, whilst Scandinavia demonstrated how trade unions could fund enterprises and government could bring together the two sides of industry. For a while, it seemed that a newly liberal corporatism had supplemented liberal democracy with economically 'functional representation' and class struggle with a socially harmonious and ethical alternative to capitalism. Having lost an empire and found a temporary role in Europe, Britain took lessons from the continent as well as from its own, socially inclined intellectuals.

MacIntyre is one such intellectual, who learned much first from socialism and then from Catholicism's social teaching and traditional, Thomist philosophy, albeit one who has never aimed to influence British Labour Party or governmental economic policy. In using MacIntyre's practical philosophy to support Pearce's proposal, Hall puts MacIntyre's work to what may be understood as a new purpose. For well over half a century he has become increasingly famous as a resolute opponent of both the modern state and capitalism, which he sees as interlinked in different ways in the USA, in western Europe, in the People's Republic of China, and even in the Soviet model of what some socialists once called 'actually-existing socialism', others called 'bureaucratic collectivism' and he still calls 'state capitalism'. As a critic of capitalism, he still refers to Marx's account of labour's exploitation and happily accepts characterization as a 'revolutionary' (albeit also 'Thomistic') Aristotelian. Nonetheless, many aspiring moral theorists of capitalism, management and human resources have attempted to use his arguments to propose relatively humane kinds of capitalist enterprise and benign kinds of management. What they still take as their philosophical and ethical warrant for so doing is the argument of MacIntyre's 1981 *After Virtue: A Study in Moral Theory*. Here, MacIntyre advanced a hostile critique of 'bureaucratic management' and of managerial 'manipulation' before taking the conceptually innovative step of distinguishing ethical, social 'practices' from organizational 'institutions', and the further, philosophical step of proposing practices, alone, as 'the first stage' in a newly social, and 'sociological', 'account of the virtues'.

In following Pearce's differentiation of the social economy as a 'third system' distinct from both 'the first system' of corporate capitalism and second system of state planning and welfare, Hall takes another path from that of those who would make MacIntyre into a new Peter Drucker. She proposes that MacIntyre provides the clearly expressed philosophy for which Pearce appeals, to articulate third-system values and a vision of how organizations and individuals might work together for the common good capable of motivating 'radical' action to bring about its actualization. Hers is indeed a more appropriate use of MacIntyre's ethical and political arguments than those which she criticises.

MacIntyre's own argument is radically social. His identification with what he has reconstructed as an Aristotelian tradition of shared, practical reasoning about goods and virtues bases even what he says of socially particular practices in an understanding of humans as dependent, rational and therefore political animals. Practices he defines as social pursuits of 'goods internal to a practice', such that the activity of pursuit is constitutive of practices and defines each distinct practice. The goods, he specifies, are of two kinds. One is the good of the product or performance at which practitioners aim, which present each practitioner with established standards of excellence to emulate. The other is the good of a particular kind of life, which, insofar as one participates in a given practice, will be constitutive of one's own good as a person and a human being. To this we may add that, in presenting persons with a conception of a good greater than oneself, practices serve as the schools of the virtues, in which individuals redirect their desires and passions toward goods that they pursue in common with others, acquiring through their practice such virtues as courage, truthfulness and justice toward one another. All of this is well elaborated by Hall.

Juxtaposed to practices are institutions. These have no goods internal or particular to them. Rather, they are power structures directed to the accumulation of such instrumental goods as power, money and social status which are external to any practice, that may be acquired in many different ways, and which tend to be zero-sum goods, so that the more there is for one, the less there will be for others. They are, therefore, goods that institutions allocate as rewards, rather than for excellence in pursuit of goods internal to any practice that the institution manages. MacIntyre, therefore, warns that institutions tend to corrupt practices, and that a primary function of the moral virtues is to sustain resistance to such corruption. Even so, these external goods are indeed good, because they are means to the achievement of further goods. As Hall well describes, *After Virtue*'s social and political argument is that goods external to practices should be used to subserve pursuit of practices' internal goods. Having parted from Marx because Marx departed from practical philosophy, and because Marxist states never 'withered away' but became labour's new expropriators, MacIntyre extended socialist critique from the proposition that capital should be made to subserve human needs and goods to the proposition that all institutions should subserve practical and common goods. Where Marx's *Capital* refers to capitalists, exploitation and ideology, *After Virtue* refers to managers, manipulation and demoralization, and to the virtues prized by a premodern tradition, and exemplified in such traditional practices as farming and fishing, sports and arts, in which internal goods and standards are well established and recognized. Pitting Aristotle against Friedrich Nietzsche, as well as against the Enlightenment's failure in moral theory upon which MacIntyre and Nietzsche concurred, and against the sociology Max Weber that Nietzsche helped inspire, MacIntyre presents modernity's characteristic, managerial institutions as vehicles for a disguised will to power. For MacIntyre, unlike Nietzsche, if moral nihilism is to be resisted, it must be through shared ethical reason and practice, not through the assertion of individual will.

With such a view, MacIntyre inspires through argumentative rigour rather than the optimism of a Pearce or Blair. Whereas others who self-identify as Aristotelians, MacIntyre refuses to credit bureaucratic nation states as instruments of any genuinely common good. Rather, he insists that a common good must be constituted by particular, productive practices, and by the practice of a participative politics of local community. His 2016 *Ethics in the Conflicts of Modernity* allows that a local political community and economy can be of considerable size, providing sophisticated forms of exchange between local producers and consumers and between them and more distant others, whilst serving the agreed purposes of their entire community. This, he proposes, has been done in Kerala in southern India, as well as in locally Communist Bologna and, at smaller scale, in such places as a Danish fishing village and a Brazilian *favela*. Such local, political economies resemble what Pearce's vision of a social economy insofar as they coexist with both capitalist corporations and a centralized state, and insofar as they depend, to some degree, upon that state for protection and resources.

Although Hall commends MacIntyre's ethical emphasis on practices and political emphasis upon locality, her own focus (like that of those commentators she criticizes) is upon the social enterprise as a new organizational form differing from that of the capitalist corporation. As she indicates, corporate businesses remain the preeminent examples of MacIntyre's critically defined institutions, crucial though states are as their principal accompaniment. Her argument is that what she, following Pearce, calls *radical* social enterprises actualize something of the ethical orientation that MacIntyre proposed back in 1981. In 2016, he (following the sociology of Tom Burns) praised collaborative effort in early years of the British Broadcasting (public) Corporation for doing the same, as that in the early years of America's private, and now multinational, Cummins Engine Company. These past exceptions to the general rule of such statist and capitalist institutional forms allow the optimistic thought that an institutional form designed with other rules, in pursuit of shared, local goals, might encourage and reward virtuous pursuit of common goods, even when the practices are as new as once were broadcasting and the manufacture of diesel engines. Here, MacIntyre might share something of the optimism of Pearce and Hall. And, as Hall suggests, such encouragement might prove all the greater where, as in Mondragon, a local culture of interacting social enterprises is able to develop.

In describing social enterprises as an institutional form that constrains the will to profit and facilitates pursuit of practices' goods and society's common good, Hall presents an ethical alternative to capitalism. Unlike the twentieth century's dominant, statist socialisms, her alternative could enable us all to exercise our shared practical rationality as what MacIntyre calls 'plain persons', diminishing our domination by institutional rationality and by the managerial 'expertise' that *After Virtue* condemns as a 'moral fiction'. In that spirit and that hope, we would all do well to follow Hall's argument.

London, UK Kelvin Knight

Acknowledgements I wish to acknowledge the support and guidance provided by Dr. Kelvin Knight and Dr. Ian Hume, I greatly appreciate your contributions to my writing. I am also deeply grateful for the encouragement from Jess, Grace and my parents, thank you for your love and influence.

Contents

CHAPTER 1

Introduction

Social Enterprise as the Model of Virtuous Business Practice?

The term social enterprise is relatively modern, in Europe it first appeared in the 1990s (Nyssens, 2006) and is used to describe an organisation which is profit generating but has a social purpose as its primary aim. As will be seen in this book, the types of organisation which can be classed as social enterprises are varied and diverse, yet they all have the overriding objective of promoting a social good. Social enterprise is considered part of the social economy because it involves trading; Pearce (2003) defines the social economy where organisations use trading to advance their social objectives. There has been increased attention given to organisations with a social purpose in recent years because they are believed to contribute to social, environmental and economic regeneration (Haugh, 2005). Social enterprises represent a key type of organisation within this sector and as such have become the subject of research into their efficacy, organisational structure and most contentiously its characterisation (Young & Lecy, 2012). However, there is a paucity of research on virtue theory in social enterprise which this book will redress through the work of Alasdair MacIntyre. Virtue theory is concerned with the qualities necessary for good character and originates in Greek philosophy, principally Aristotle. It is my contention that when the organisational structure, social purpose and historical antecedents to social enterprise are analysed, they will reveal

G. Hall, *Virtue and Social Enterprise*,
https://doi.org/10.1007/978-3-031-14027-3_1

that it represents a virtuous organisation as understood by MacIntyre. In pursuit of this aim, MacIntyre's work on virtues, practice, institutions and tradition will play a central role in analysing the potential for virtue in social enterprises. Furthermore, the virtue-practice-institution framework developed by Geoff Moore and Ron Beadle, and their work on the institution housing the practice and their view of a virtuous organisation will be used in the context of social enterprise. If social enterprises as trading organisations with a social purpose can be considered virtuous organisations, this will add weight to the view held here that social enterprises represent the model of best practice for a business type organisation in terms of their community benefits, sustainable use of resources and their economic and social contribution to the good of society.

Aims of the Book

Following from the above, my aims are to demonstrate that social enterprise can represent a virtuous organisation and moreover, that radical social enterprise can represent a viable alternative to the capitalist business model. To accomplish this, consideration needs to be given to the historical antecedents to social enterprise and their influence on current practice. The tradition of thought accumulated through its history and structural integrity of the modern social enterprise give an indication of the potential for such organisations to demonstrate a path to virtue. The historical antecedents to social enterprise give a fuller understanding of the possibilities of a virtue-based organisation. Born out of the social and cooperative movements in industrial Europe (Nyssens, 2006), social enterprises represent a potentially virtuous business organisation that does not need to maximise profits as its primary goal and is motivated by social goods. The social enterprise is distinct from mainstream business because it identifies with a tradition of thought from the third sector which is distinct from private and public sectors of the economy and is focused on contributing to the common goods in society (the three sectors or systems of the economy will be discussed in greater detail in Chapter 6). Social enterprises share a common understanding of their role within society through their history, which guides the pursuit of practices and internal goods accordingly. They are positioned in communities with objectives to address social problems within that community; MacIntyre (1999) posits that common goods can be achieved through such an intermediary institution which is neither the state nor the family. There is research into virtue ethics in business, most notably by Moore who has developed characteristics for a virtuous corporation. Whilst such characteristics may arguably improve the ethical behaviour in business, they do not address the fundamental purpose of generating profit. Whereas social enterprises are committed to their social purpose, first and foremost, whilst generating a profit only to continue the social good. I will argue that a shared practical reasoning and understanding of common goods and how they relate to internal goods will distinguish social enterprises as not only distinct from mainstream business, but also a virtuous alternative in accordance with MacIntyre's views of a practice and institution. The historical antecedents to social enterprise will provide an explanation of the 'road to virtue' for this type of organisation. Radical social enterprises are distinguished from reformist social enterprises by John Pearce (2003) as the former rejects capitalism whilst the latter supports the existing system, including capitalism. I will argue that radical social enterprises can represent a viable alternative to capitalism with MacIntyre's work providing a philosophical basis for such a theory. Pearce's radical social enterprise will be developed in greater detail than originally specified by Pearce, to construct a conceptual scheme which identifies the relationship between virtue according to MacIntyre and the radical social enterprise envisaged by Pearce.

MacIntyre's Virtue and Its Application to Social Enterprise

Virtue ethics relies on a person's character as the means of assessing ethical behaviour and virtue, rather than judging actions based on universal rights and duties, or by the outcomes or consequences of an action (Blackburn, 2008). Alasdair MacIntyre is one of the key writers on modern virtue ethics and his work will form a central focus for the compatibility of social enterprise with virtue. MacIntyre develops the idea in *After Virtue* (2007) that modern liberal society has a fragmented moral view because we have an incomplete understanding of morality and ethics because vital theory and terminology dating back to Greek philosophy has been lost through the ages. Thus, any moral framework in which coherent ethical choices and decisions could be made has also been lost. MacIntyre employs Aristotelian theories of telos or purpose as the missing source of moral instruction. Individuals are able to pursue their role virtuously in society through the application of reason, which is achieved through practice and can enable human flourishing. The attainment of virtues through practice is a central theme in MacIntyre's work. Indeed, the virtues are primarily, although not exclusively achieved through developing excellence in practice. MacIntyre (2007) describes a practice as a cooperative human activity in which the participants strive to achieve excellence, as defined by that activity. MacIntyre (2007) defines internal goods as being achieved through striving to excel in a chosen practice and are specific to that practice. However, external goods are contingently linked to a practice and can always be achieved through other means and therefore not specifically assigned to a practice. According to MacIntyre, an institution is necessary for the pursuit of practices, for example, a hospital is the institution which houses the practice of medicine and provides the necessary environment for the pursuit of excellence in the practice. The practice of medicine requires the commitment and dedication to excellence by its practitioners to perform their duties, but also involves the advancement of the practice through new techniques and cures for illnesses. Thus, internal goods are created through the pursuit of excellence in the practice of medicine. The hospital as the institution is responsible for the creation of external goods such as income to ensure that the hospital has the financial means to enable the medical practitioners to perform their duties to such levels of excellence. However, MacIntyre recognises a tension between the priorities of internal goods of excellence and external goods because there is always the danger of internal goods being compromised by the acquisitiveness of institutional avarice. This type of tension can occur when an excessive focus is given by the institution to acquiring external goods such as prestige or money, which can be at the expense of the practice. Thus, in the example of the hospital, where there is excessive focus on income generation which is not for the benefit of the practitioners and instead employed for other uses such as payment in dividends to shareholders or excessive bureaucratic management structure, there is potential for the internal goods associated with the practice to suffer. For MacIntyre, there can be no balancing of priorities if the virtues are to be achieved, there is a hierarchical ranking of goods in which external goods are subordinate to internal goods. MacIntyre uses the example of two fishing crews, one which values purely economic ends and the other which values the skills and excellence associated with fishing and being a crew member. In the latter example, crew members will support each other and their fishing community through difficulties because their aim is the excellence associated with their work. Whereas the crew which prioritises purely economic ends will be focused on individual reward and will develop skills to achieve such rewards (MacIntyre, 1994). Thus, the crew striving for excellence will prioritise internal goods such as excellence in fishing and maintaining a sustainable source of fish, whereas the economic crew will be focused on external goods such as financial reward, without the commitment to sustainable fishing or the long-term health of the industry.

For MacIntyre, the focus for an institution should be the internal goods, with external goods subordinated to them and only pursued for the purposes of maintaining the practice housed by the institution. He argues that a practice has a community of practitioners who are dedicated to a common pursuit in their practice and each contributes to a common goal in extending that practice. For MacIntyre, goods are achieved through a communal understanding and approach to virtue. He is highly critical of the modern economy and writes that modernity has lost the understanding of virtue through a focus on individualism. Lutz (2012), in his interpretation of MacIntyre, argues that the virtues have become meaningless, without the context of the common good and teleology. For MacIntyre, a teleological approach is essential to create the social conditions which facilitate achievement of the human good. The teleological approach enables the rank ordering of goods through a hierarchy in which external goods are subordinated to practices' internal goods. That is the subordination of external goods allows the facilitation of excellence in practice which, in turn, allows the acquisition of the virtues.

MacIntyre (2007) asserts that to understand and pursue goods and excellence through practice, we must also understand the context in which we live in terms of our shared tradition of community and culture. Tradition plays a key role for MacIntyre in which the virtues are pursued through practice, with an understanding of the history in which those practices have evolved and the historical context in which communal society operates. Furthermore, it is through striving for excellence in practice that we maintain the historical significance of the traditions in both our lives and in the practices. It is not sufficient to simply carry out a practice; excellence or virtue is the goal when engaged in a practice, but crucially the practice is also embedded in the tradition and history derived from the community in which the practice is found. Therefore, MacIntyre asserts that all practices have their own history in relation to those practitioners who have extended the knowledge and excellence in that practice up to the present. Furthermore, current practitioners will continue to extend their practice in this way for future practitioners; thus, an historical element is critical to a proper understanding of virtues (MacIntyre, 2007). Thus, it is not just about the individual or individuals, it is about the history and development of that particular community. Individuals are able to flourish in the pursuit of excellence in their practice which benefits their community through its development and advancement. Also, presumably, those individuals have benefitted from the contributions of those in its history and development.

MacIntyre's practice and institution will be considered in relation to social enterprise and his views on the importance of history and tradition will be considered in the context of the antecedents to social enterprise. Social enterprise is a relatively modern term for an organisation which has a social purpose yet is profit-making; it is borne of a collective history of cooperatives, community enterprises, labour movements and social unrest which have all had an impact on the modern social enterprise (Nyssens, 2006). In examining MacIntyre's views on tradition and history, it is the intention to demonstrate the influence of these predecessors to social enterprises and identify virtue through their influence. The forebears to the social enterprise can be traced back through voluntary and cooperative activities which were set up to address a variety of social ills, such as lack of habitable housing, medical care and affordable goods.[1] In the UK, the Industrial Revolution brought a significant change to the nation, both in terms of the working environment and in terms of the social structure of the labouring classes. The Industrial Revolution cultivated a capitalist economy, dominated by an emphasis on profit with workers who mostly owned nothing except their labour. Hobsbawm (1999) describes all life and the economy as being dominated by the capitalist drive for profits. The resulting poor pay and conditions prevailing in industries which appeared and expanded during this period is symptomatic of this profit-maximising motive. Indeed, this trend can be seen in major capitalist nations today. For example, in the UK 14.3 million individuals (one-fifth of the nation) now live in poverty and 4.1 million children live

[1] The Rochdale Equitable Pioneers Society was established in 1844 selling unadulterated food at fair prices. It is recognised as the founder of co-operativism by the International Co-operative Alliance (Ridley-Duff & Bull, 2016, p. 24).

in poverty. There has been a dramatic rise in UK poverty since 2011/12 and this rise has been greatest for working individuals. For children, the rise has been greatest for those with a working parent (Barnard, 2018). In her report for the Joseph Rowntree Foundation, Barnard also gives details of the negative impact for those living in poverty regarding their health and wellbeing. For example, Matthews-King (2019) reports that 'Dickensian' diseases and illnesses in children have dramatically increased since 2010. And yet The Equality Trust (2018) reports that during the period examined by Barnard (2018) (2013–2018), the UK's 1000 wealthiest individuals have increased their wealth by £274 billion to a total wealth of £724 billion.

Reeve et al. (2004) note that as a consequence of the Industrial Revolution and resulting poverty, there was drive by social reformers to redress the exploitation of the workforce by capitalists, using a sense of moral responsibility. The result of this was the increasing popularity or necessity of movements which attempted to promote and improve the conditions of the poorest in society. These movements vary throughout the period from the beginning of the Industrial Revolution to the present day, but nevertheless maintain a similar priority regarding the meeting of social needs. The cooperative movement was one such movement, based on the ethical principles of self-help, mutual support and democratic involvement (Potter, 1904). The argument here is that social enterprise viewed in the context of its history will create a fuller understanding of the potential for practices within such organisations, thus enabling an exploration of virtue within modern social enterprise as understood by MacIntyre. Furthermore, social enterprises are often associated with communities where members of a particular community have established a social enterprise to meet common needs in that community, such as community radio, which will be considered in relation to MacIntyre's view that certain communities enable virtues to flourish. Indeed, MacIntyre views the common goods of community as essential to a practice (Knight, 1998) and argues that common goods must be understood prior to individual goods; it is only through goods collectively pursued that we come to understand what our individual goods are (MacIntyre, 2007). MacIntyre (2016) suggests that a political community is necessary to organise and achieve the common goods of a community which engages in shared deliberation and he identifies the elements of a politics of making and sustaining local communities. I argue that the elements needed for such a local community are incorporated within the structure and operation of a radical social enterprise and as such, they are able to contribute to developing the common goods of community. MacIntyre suggests that cooperatives demonstrate the virtues needed to achieve the common goods of community and encourage their flourishing. However, I will argue that radical social enterprises envisioned by Pearce represent a broader application of MacIntyre's virtues through common goods of community than cooperatives alone.

MacIntyre, Business and Capitalism

There are attempts to apply MacIntyre's virtues and practices to business institutions, most notably by Moore who has written extensively about the subject (2002, 2005a, 2005b, 2008, 2012a, 2012b, 2015, 2017, Hirschman, 1982; Maitland, 1997; Warren, 1996). Moore argues that it is possible to create virtuous businesses within the UK and US capitalist system where the organisation has a good or just purpose (2012b). However, I contend that capitalist institutions are focused on external goods and do not abide by the hierarchical ordering of goods in accordance with MacIntyre, which is to the detriment of the virtues. Thus, an exploration of the research on MacIntyre's work in relation to capitalist business will be presented to determine whether they are compatible.

Moore developed a set of virtuous corporate characteristics using MacIntyre's writings on virtue which, he argued, if in place in an organisation, would create the ideally virtuous organisation. Moore (2005b) argues that his positive application of virtue theory to business has the capacity to improve business and also explain the tensions inherent in organisational purpose. According to Moore, his analysis provides meaningful insights into the development of virtues in business and greatly improves the understanding of virtues in a corporate context. Moore recognises that for a virtuous organisation to align with MacIntyre's view it would require that practice and excellence have priority within the institution, with external goods such as profit being a consequence of excellence in practice. Also, that external goods such as profit should only be focused on to the extent required to maintain and develop the practice. MacIntyre holds that external goods are an unintentional benefit in the pursuit of excellence in a practice and therefore should not be a priority over the practice. Moore recognises the flaw in business organisations excessively pursuing external goods and argues they must avoid the tendency towards greed. Keat (2008) argues that MacIntyre views capitalism as incompatible with his views on practices and virtues. Furthermore, Beadle (2002) argues that capitalist businesses are concerned with effectiveness, rather than excellence which is at odds with MacIntyrean practices and the pursuit of excellence. It is my contention that capitalist business is not capable of being aligned with MacIntyre's view of institutions where the virtues are nurtured through practices, because capitalism is founded on liberal individualism in which individuals pursue their own interests without first conceptualising a common good. Equally, MacIntyre would not ascribe practices as being virtuous any more than he would institutions, because virtues are only attributable to humans. Furthermore, I will argue in this book that capitalist businesses do not subscribe to a rank ordering of goods in which external goods such as wealth and prestige are subordinate to the internal goods of practices and are therefore unable to be aligned with MacIntyre's views on virtue. To fully embrace the pursuit of virtues such as justice, courage and honesty according to MacIntyre's account, it is essential to firstly value their role in society. I argue that any conception of capitalist business as being in accord with MacIntyre is flawed for this reason because capitalist business favours the external goods of wealth and prestige and has created organisational structures which support such a focus, which will be explored in greater detail throughout this book. The decision-making process in capitalist organisations excludes the labour force in favour of decision-making based on efficiency. In contrast, Pearce's radical social enterprises are run by the labour force and use capital to pursue the common ends determined by their founding purpose. Their institutional structures are developed to ensure such things as democratic decision-making which enable the shared discussion of common goods. Thus, radical social enterprises subordinate external goods to the primary purpose of achieving social or common goods.

I will argue that capitalism is unfit for creating such virtuous organisations because it is fundamentally based on accumulation of wealth, through the most efficient and effective use of labour. They are structured to ensure power and control is in the hands of the owners of capital and their representatives. MacIntyre (2016) asserts the importance of the power balance and decision-making structure in the institution and its ability to develop practices. He identifies cooperatives as a type of organisation which could encourage practices through devolved ownership and control, which will also be explored within this book. I also consider the alternatives to capitalist organisations which exist, that operate using shared decision-making and focus on common goods, whilst only creating profits for the purposes of continuing the organisation, rather than making external goods the priority.

Alternative Forms of Business

Whilst capitalism may be antithetical to MacIntyrean practices, there are alternative forms of market-based organisations which could be more attuned to his views and more akin to the cooperatives he explores in *Ethics in the Conflicts of Modernity* (2016). There are institutions which operate within market systems that do not conform to capitalist pursuit of profit in the same manner. Moore's virtuous organisation characteristics are useful in determining the types of organisations which may be compatible with MacIntyre. Moore (2005b) cites the practice and excellence as primary goals, together with a just purpose, power-balanced structure and a culture which supports the virtues of fortitude, temperance, justice, prudence and integrity. However, MacIntyre's practice definition forms part of his wider views on the role of common goods and political community in achieving the virtues. Practices, for MacIntyre, must form part of a community in which there is a shared understanding of common goods to be pursued through cooperative activity. The social centre movement in the UK is deemed to typify practice-based communities according to Finchett-Maddock (2008) because the focus is on living outside of consumer society and rejecting capitalism.[2] Dawson and Bartholomew (2003) argue that trade, rather than profits, is needed for the exchange of goods in communities; exchange and barter predate the inclusion of profit in trade transactions. Their argument reveals the potential for a broader range of organisations which rely on alternative forms of exchange, including volunteer labour, which also contribute to the common good of the community. Indeed, MacIntyre's (2007) view of capitalism and modernity is that it is inimical to community sustenance and virtues because they encourage a lack of shared understanding of what would constitute a community good. Blackledge (2009) argues that capitalism prevents the virtues and the development of communities through the deliberate misunderstanding that external goods and their

[2] The social centre movement supports the creation of social centres as community spaces which serve the needs of the community.

acquisition equate to success. MacIntyre (2016) refers to cooperatives and community initiatives when discussing the importance of common goods in the development of virtues and the role of local politics in attaining common goods. The cooperative characteristics according to Reeve et al. (2004) share important features with MacIntyre's elements for creating a politics of making and sustaining local communities and the common good. Shared deliberation and the power-balance amongst members with a common understanding of the goods to be achieved suggest a harmony between cooperatives and MacIntyre's community flourishing. MacIntyre views cooperatives as representative of a practice embodying institution[3] which are community based. However, as we shall see, there are other organisational forms such as social enterprises which may also represent such an institution and be compatible with MacIntyre.

Defining Social Enterprise

A social enterprise is an organisation which is profit-making but its primary function is to further a social good. There are a variety of organisations which can be defined as social enterprises, ranging from credit unions to worker's cooperatives. In the UK, social enterprises are considered to be organisations which use trading to enable the furtherance of their social objectives. Research in the USA focuses on a business-like structure, but also with a broad range of forms such as cooperatives, social firms and voluntary organisations. In mainland Europe, research has highlighted a greater emphasis on the cooperative nature of social enterprise (Nyssens, 2006). Indeed, it was in Italy that the concept of a social enterprise was first established in 1990, following the cooperative initiatives which had developed in the late 1980s (Nyssens, 2006). The main characteristic of the cooperative being the shared responsibilities and benefits between members, with legal structures tending to emphasise the stakeholder role in governance to ensure that all those with an interest in the organisation are considered, rather than only the shareholders. However, it could be argued that to focus only on the legal frameworks for social enterprise is a very limited view of a broad range of enterprises which largely do not hold any legal definition for their activities. There are many organisations which can be deemed social enterprise because of their social

[3] MacIntyre uses the term 'practice embodying institution' (1994, p. 290).

function, rather than their legal status and it is this variety of form which characterise social enterprises as a sector much more than a legal definition (Pearce, 2003; Ridley-Duff & Bull, 2016; Young & Lecy, 2012).

Following from the above controversies about the meaning of social enterprise, there have been a variety of attempts to classify social enterprise, ranging from comparisons of form (Esposito, 2012; Kerlin, 2006) to a typology of social enterprise (Alter, 2010). Emerging from such research are several schools of thought which attempt to characterise the social enterprise. They include an ideal-type organisation in which there are a set of key characteristics or principles to which a social enterprise should aspire (Spear & Bidet, 2003); a spectrum of organisational types which incorporates organisations with some form of social purpose, ranging from profit maximising, socially responsible businesses to charities (Alter, 2010); a social innovation emphasis in which social goals are achieved through entrepreneurial activities, with no defining organisational form (Young, 1983); and a 'zoo' analogy focusing on diversity in which commercial and social interests intersect in many different guises (Young & Lecy, 2012). However, one of the central arguments of this book is that these studies, while aiming to create a practical framework in which social enterprises may be categorised and measured, fail to properly consider the underlying values and tradition of this type of organisation. My contention here is that to understand the modern social enterprise, it is necessary to explore its predecessors, which can provide valuable insights into the motivations and values underlying such organisations. My integration of social enterprise with MacIntyre's views on practice and tradition will provide the basis for exploring the virtues in social enterprise. It is further argued that radical social enterprise is more akin to McIntyre's views and removes the ambiguity realised by the above authors regarding what constitutes a social enterprise and the disparate models that have been proposed. Indeed, once the core definitions of social enterprises are considered (later in Chapter 5); it will be seen that radical social enterprise, as proposed by Pearce, is more akin to this consensus than reformist social enterprise.

The EMES International Research Network (EMES) has developed a large body of research into the field of social enterprise in Europe and is a valuable source of reference in understanding the context and structures in which social enterprises operate. The ideal-type model is the approach taken by EMES through its research into the emergence of social enterprise and its characteristics. The EMES research posits that social enterprise is rooted in the social economy, also referred to as the third sector, in which the principles of mutuality and meeting social needs over profit maximising are core. According to Defourny (2010), the term social economy is an historical concept which dates back to the nineteenth century during the Industrial Revolution. The inclusion of social enterprise within the social economy has been viewed as a new dynamic in the sector, different from non-profit organisations and yet still retaining the conceptual integrity of organisations typical to the third sector. Laville and Nyssens (2001) suggest that social enterprises represent the possibility of alternative forms of solidarity-based economic transactions using the principles of solidarity, cooperation, participation and reciprocity and could be a realistic alternative to wealth focused business. The European Commission's Social Economy Unit included social enterprises in its definition of the social economy, thus aligning them with the key principles of social economy organisations which includes putting community before profit (Defourny & Beveltere, 1999).

To facilitate the understanding of the dynamics of social enterprise Laville and Nyssens (2001) applied a tripolar analysis of socio-economic organisation; the three aspects included the structure of ownership, social capital and the distribution of economic goods and services. This approach served as a means of exploring the key dimensions of social enterprise to reach an understanding of the rationale of such organisations. Furthermore, the EMES research network established a set of characteristics for social enterprise which included key elements such as an explicit aim to benefit the community, limits to profit distribution, a high degree of autonomy in decision-making and decision-making powers not based on capital ownership and stakeholder participation.

The EMES research offers a comprehensive definition of the key characteristics of a social enterprise in its ideal form, which are essential to understanding the organisational structure and an indication of its priorities and values. However, as noted above, I contend that social enterprises have an underlying tradition of thought which cannot be understood or articulated in a set of characteristics or on a spectrum, or any of the methods previously identified. To fully understand the values and possibly the virtues inherent to a social enterprise, it is necessary to explore the historical antecedents to the modern social enterprise. It is through such an approach that the virtues and their influence in social enterprise can be fully explored. As noted above, Pearce contributed to the social enterprise field of study and identified two types of social enterprise in the forms of radical and reformist in which the former rejects capitalism and the latter supports the organisations within capitalism. Pearce's work has been further developed more recently by Alan Kay, Michael J. Roy and Cam Donaldson in the article *Re-imagining social enterprise* (2016).

Contextualising Pearce's Social Enterprise

Pearce (2003) presents social enterprise as part of the wider economy and distinguishes the different elements as first, second and third systems, according to their values. The first system represents profit-oriented business, the second system represents the public sector and the third, social purpose. Pearce argues that there are key characteristics and values which identify social enterprises from other types of organisations. Pearce acknowledges that the values associated with social enterprise are too vague and need a clearly expressed philosophy to ensure that they can make a practical difference in society. It is to this end that this book aspires, whereby MacIntyre's work could provide such a philosophical understanding for social enterprise and in particular, radical social enterprise. Pearce situates social enterprises within the third system which incorporates the social economy. The social economy, according to Pearce, is formed through community-led organisations and grass-roots organisations such as social enterprises and is founded on institutional democracy, the common good, people before profit and local community which has a regard for the environment. Social enterprises, according to Pearce, have a social purpose, are non-profit distributing and are democratically run. Pearce argues that democracy is a much wider concept in social enterprise than solely voting rights; he argues that social enterprises encourage a wider participation in the community. The values that underpin social enterprise according to Pearce include cooperation, decentralisation of power and decision-making to the lowest possible level in the community, inclusivity for all, without discrimination of any kind, good work which is socially useful and sustainability in terms of the organisation and the environment. A synthesis of the values and characteristics of social enterprise, with MacIntyre's virtue theory, will clarify the extent to which the two views are compatible. Furthermore, as noted above, Pearce identifies between radical and reformist social enterprise and it is the radical form which rejects capitalism that represents the most appropriate relationship with MacIntyre because of his views on capitalism and its influence on the attainment of virtues. The reformist social enterprise according to Pearce acts in a supporting role to capitalist business and the government by providing support in communities where neither the state nor private enterprise are willing to play a role, for example, a community cafe which helps people with mental health issues. Pearce suggests that it is not possible for reformist social enterprises to change the existing capitalist system whilst also collaborating with it, whereas radical social enterprise rejects capitalism and actively seeks ways of creating a viable alternative.

Coexist is a social enterprise in the UK which could be deemed radical and is studied in detail by Larner (2014) and provides a valuable source of evidence for understanding the radical social enterprise. In a reversal of the capitalist approach to profits and wealth, Kay et al. (2016) argue that social enterprises use economic activity to achieve their social purpose, rather than as an end as in capitalist business. They argue that economic activity in social enterprise should contribute to the wellbeing of the community where prosperity is distinct from wealth and profits. Akin to MacIntyre's politics of making and sustaining local communities, Pearce (2003) argues for a political role for social enterprise in which they represent a viable alternative to capitalism. Radical social enterprise can be viewed as part of a wider movement of organisations which are attempting to alter the dominance of capitalism towards an emphasis on community, common goods and sustainable use of resources. The dominance of capitalism is such that it is difficult to imagine alternatives according to Gibson-Graham (2006) and therefore it is essential to promote the alternatives. MacIntyre's work on virtues and flourishing could provide the necessary philosophical understanding for radical social enterprise to be viewed as a viable alternative to capitalism. To determine the extent to which radical social enterprise is compatible with MacIntyre's theory requires a synthesis of both areas of study.

Through a detailed analysis of the literature relating to MacIntyre and Pearce, common themes will be identified to capture the parallels between the two areas of study. These themes will be considered in greater detail to determine whether radical social enterprise can be viewed as a realisation of MacIntyre's philosophical work. Furthermore, the radical form of social enterprise will be developed beyond Pearce's description of a social enterprise which rejects capitalism, to apply a philosophical understanding that was previously lacking. Important to both MacIntyre and radical social enterprise is the role of capitalism in its inability to develop common goods and in particular for MacIntyre, the inability of individuals to pursue the virtues. The virtues are necessary, according to MacIntyre for society to flourish, which can best be achieved through local communities, with individuals taking a political role in ensuring common goods are pursued. The role of radical social enterprise, as conceived by Pearce, could, therefore, represent an institutional form which encourages engagement with local community towards achieving common goods and individual flourishing.

The foundation of this book is MacIntyre's conception of virtues and his definition of a practice and institution. MacIntyre defines a practice as a socially cooperative activity in which practitioners strive for excellence and in the process achieve internal goods particular to the practice. Internal goods being those goods which are distinctive of the practice and can only be realised through a dedication to the pursuit of excellence in the practice (MacIntyre, 2007). It will be argued that radical social enterprises contribute to the common good through their social activities and are radical in the MacIntyrean sense through its participants promoting the idea of a wider, and locally political, common good. Radical social enterprises support practices and encourage the virtues through their institutional form. It will be argued that it is through shared deliberation by the participants in radical social enterprises who use their practical reasoning to determine their goods, which leads to a distinction between goods internal and external to shared practices so that the latter may be intentionally subordinated to the former. Pearce views the radical approach as representing an alternative economic system based on shared values and primacy of people over capital. Kay et al. (2016) in re-imagining Pearce's view of social enterprise suggest that radical social enterprise use economic activities such as profit-making towards the end, which is the social outcome as good; the economic activity is not, therefore, an end in itself; prosperity is related to wellbeing and the good of the community and not based on wealth or economic gain. Furthermore, those individuals participating in radical social enterprises understand the importance of common goods and value the role of virtues above such external goods as money, prestige and wealth. External goods associated with maintaining the practice are achieved through income generation in a radical social enterprise, but the core purpose is the achievement of common goods and internal goods specific to the enterprise. The common good can be understood in the context of the wider community through MacIntyre's (2016) explanation of the overall good for a person; it is through participation with those who we share a community, in our various practices that we are able to order our own goods towards our overall purpose. Furthermore, radical social enterprises contribute to attempts to form local political communities and can be the focal point for such attempts through their activities and their methods of decision-making which encourage shared discussion and deliberation on the common goods to be achieved. Radical social enterprises are often set up as a hub for a variety of activities which support the common good with decision-making being a cooperative process in which there is little or no hierarchy in the power structure and as such can be viewed as politically radical in the MacIntyrean sense. Institutions according to MacIntyre can prioritise external goods, to the detriment of the practices, particularly in capitalist institutions in the free market system where external goods of wealth accumulation by the owners of capital are primary. Social enterprises have been identified as part of the capitalist system by theorists such as Dees (1996) who argue that social enterprises are on a spectrum of business organisations which range from corporations who engage with corporate social responsibility to charitable organisations, with social enterprise towards the charitable side of the spectrum. Pearce (2003) identifies social enterprises as separate from what he describes as the first system of private enterprise and more with the third system in which families, communities and charities are the focus, as such, they do not conform with the capitalist mode of operation in the same way as capitalist organisations. Following from this understanding, I argue that radical social enterprises are attempting to create communities which value the common good above individualism and have a regard for the virtues, which is akin to MacIntyre's description of an institutional form within communities which develop the virtues in their approach to social and political issues. MacIntyre (1999) argues that economic considerations must be subordinated to social considerations, for a community to prosper. It will be argued that radical social enterprises are communities of people who embody the three conditions that MacIntyre argues are necessary for individual and common goods to be achieved. The conditions are shared deliberation in an institutional form, just generosity and a political structure which ensures that all have a voice. MacIntyre refers to the 'intermediate area' between the state and family in which such relationships encourage the virtue of just generosity and the understanding of the common good; it will be argued that radical social enterprises represent such an intermediate area.

Potential of the Social Enterprise Model

If the growth in the number of social enterprises were to continue and expand (Kay, 2018), there is potential for the principles of cooperation, solidarity, participation and reciprocity, which are arguably associated with social enterprise, to have a greater influence over society. MacIntyre's critique of modernity focuses on the problems of individualism being promoted in society, which leads to a lack of understanding of our place within the context of our community. The claim here is that a society with greater numbers of social enterprises could potentially refocus awareness and understanding towards more common goods and help to develop the virtues.

Outline of Chapters

Chapter 2 explores MacIntyre's view on virtue to establish a coherent grounding for understanding the role of the virtues and how they may be achieved. He makes clear the relationship and tension between internal and external goods and how, despite external goods still being goods, can have a corrupting influence on the pursuit of the internal goods associated with a practice. Furthermore, the role of common goods is shown to be inexorably linked to practices in that they are prior to individual goods; without an understanding and pursuit of the common goods, it is not possible to realise individual goods. It is as independent practical reasoners that we learn to cooperate with others to achieve our common goods but acknowledged dependence and just generosity are essential virtues to developing our common goods. The institution and how it supports the practice which it houses is seen as fundamental to the practice.

Chapter 3 aims determine if business can be considered either as a practice or as an institution which sustains practices in accordance with MacIntyre. It is argued that liberal capitalism encourages an organisational structure in which owners control capital and make decisions based on effectiveness, rather than excellence to achieve greater capital accumulation. The research on virtuous businesses is considered in which it is argued that businesses which can demonstrate the correct balance between internal and external goods can be virtuous.

Chapter 4 continues with the analysis of virtues in business and considers whether internal goods are prioritised over external goods in the hierarchical approach of MacIntyre. Further, alternative forms of institutions, including cooperatives and social enterprises, are considered and the extent to which they exhibit commitment to these key elements of MacIntyre's work.

Chapter 5 looks at the ways in which researchers have defined social enterprise and identifies the common aspects. There is particular focus on the ideal type and spectrum approaches to social enterprise as these are the more widely researched. It is noted that the spectrum approach highlights the possibility for a balance or trade off to occur when determining what MacIntyre would term internal and external goods. It is, therefore, argued that a more radical form of social enterprise should be explored to determine the commitment to a rank order of goods. Pearce's (2003) two alternative views of social enterprise, termed 'reformist' and 'radical', are then considered in detail. Here it will be seen that the reformist approach engages with capitalism and attempts to improve and reform it from within. Whilst radical social enterprises reject capitalism, consistent with MacIntyre and also aligns with MacIntyre's hierarchical structuring of goods to ensure the social purpose is paramount.

In Chapter 6, the third system, also referred to as the social economy, is explored in greater detail to create a landscape for understanding social enterprise and the values that underpin such organisations. Radical and reformist social enterprises are discussed to highlight the distinction between them and create a framework to elaborate further on radical social enterprise. The social and political context will be considered to identify the influences on radical social enterprise and explore the implications of their existence and growth on the wider economy. Pearce only refers briefly to the radical form of social enterprise, which in my view is the most appropriate form of social enterprise to reflect MacIntyre's virtue theory. Therefore, this chapter and the next will fully develop the characteristics of a radical social enterprise so that it can be analysed against MacIntyre.

In Chapter 7, Pearce's social enterprise characteristics and values and MacIntyre's views on virtue, practice and institution are synergised to create a framework for radical social enterprise. It is argued that the characteristics and values which Pearce identifies indicate an affinity to

MacIntyre through a social purpose which has priority over external goods. Moreover, the outcome of the synthesis leads to the argument that radical social enterprises are a clearer and less ambiguous representation of MacIntyre's view of a common good-supporting institution compared to the more general promotion of cooperative organisations as propagated by him. It is also argued that radical social enterprises are more consistent with an outright rejection of capitalism which is necessary to create the kind of radical change promoted by both Pearce and MacIntyre. Finally, it is argued that through the synthesis of these two authors, a more specific understanding of the shared values of radical social enterprise can be understood and promoted.

The final chapter argues that radical social enterprise has been shown to represent a MacIntyrean institution in which common goods and internal goods are achieved through practices, with a commitment to finding an alternative to capitalism. Furthermore, they can be viewed as radical in a MacIntyrean sense because they promote the idea of a locally political common good through encouraging participation in local political communities in which common goods can be determined.

References

Alter, K. (2010). *Social enterprise typology*. http://www.4lenses.org/setypology (Accessed 20 September 2016).

Barnard, H. (2018). *UK poverty 2018: A comprehensive analysis of poverty trends and figures*. Joseph Rowntree Foundation.

Beadle, R. (2002). The misappropriation of MacIntyre. *Reason in Practice, 2*, 45–54.

Blackburn, S. (2008). *Oxford dictionary of philosophy*. Oxford University Press.

Blackledge, P. (2009). Alasdair MacIntyre: Social practices marxism and ethical anti-capitalism. *Political Studies, 57*(4), 866–884. https://doi.org/10.1111/j.1467-9248.2008.00770.x

Dawson, D., & Bartholomew, C. (2003). Virtues, managers and business people: Finding a place for MacIntyre in a business context. *Journal of Business Ethics, 48*, 127–138.

Dees, G. (1996). *The social enterprise spectrum: Philanthropy to commerce*. Harvard Business School, Publishing Division.

Defourny, J. (2010). *Social economy*. https://emes.net/index.php?id (Accessed January 2010).

Defourny, J., & Beveltere, P. (1999). *The social economy: The worldwide making of a third sector*.

EMES International Research Network. http://emes.net/index.php?id=203 (Accessed 14 February 2010).

Esposito, R. T. (2012). The social enterprise revolution in corporate law: A primer on hybrid corporate entities in Europe and the United States and the case for the benefit corporation. *William & Mary Business Law Review, 4*(2), 639–714.

Finchett-Maddock, L. (2008). An anarchist's wetherspoons or virtuous resistance? Social centres as MacIntyre's vision of practice-based communities. *Philosophy of Management, 7*(1), 21–31.

Gibson-Graham, J. K. (2006). *The end of capitalism (as we knew it): A feminist critique of political economy*. University of Minnesota Press.

Haugh, H. (2005). A research agenda for social entrepreneurship. *Social Enterprise Journal, 1*(1), 1–12.

Hirschman, A. (1982). Rival interpretations of market society: Civilising, destructive, or feeble? *Journal of Economic Literature, 20*(4), 1463–1484.

Hobsbawm, E. (1999). *Industry and empire*. Penguin Books Ltd.

Kay, L. (2018). *Social enterprises 'contribute £60bn to the economy each year'*. https://www.thirdsector.co.uk/social-enterprises (Accessed June 2022).

Kay, A., Roy, M. J., & Donaldson, C. (2016). Re-imagining social enterprise. *Social Enterprise Journal, 12*(2), 217–234.

Keat, R. (2008). Practices, firms and varieties of capitalism. *Philosophy of Management, 7*(1), 77–91.

Kerlin, J. (2006). Social enterprise in the United States and Europe: Understanding and learning from the differences. *VOLUNTAS: International Journal of Voluntary and Nonprofit Organizations, 17*(3), 246–262.

Knight, K. (1998). *The MacIntyre reader*. Polity Press.

Larner, W. (2014). The limits of post-politics: Rethinking radical social enterprise. In J. Wilson & E. Swyngedouw (Eds.), *The post-political and its discontents: Spaces of depoliticisation, spectres of radical politics*. Edinburgh University Press.

Laville, J.-L., & Nyssens, M. (2001). The social enterprise: Towards a theoretical socio-economic approach. In C. Borzaga & J. Defourny (Eds.), *The emergence of social enterprise*. Routledge.

Lutz, C. S. (2012). *Reading Alasdair MacIntyre's after virtue*. Continuum International Publishing Group.

MacIntyre, A. (1994). A partial response to my critics. In J. Horton & S. Mendus (Eds.), *After MacIntyre* (pp. 283–304). Polity Press.

MacIntyre, A. (1999). *Dependent rational animals: Why human beings need the virtues*. Carus Publishing Company.

MacIntyre, A. (2007). *After virtue* (3rd ed.). University of Notre Dame Press.

MacIntyre, A. (2016). *Ethics in the conflicts of modernity: An essay on desire, practical reasoning and narrative*. Cambridge University Press.

Maitland, I. (1997). Virtuous markets: The market as school of the virtues. *Business Ethics Quarterly, 7*(1), 7–31.
Matthews-King, A. (2019, February 2). 'Dickensian' diseases on the rise under Tory-led governments: From scarlet fever to tuberculosis to malnutrition. *Independent*.
Moore, G. (2002). On the implications of the practice-institution distinction: MacIntyre and the application of modern virtue ethics to business. *Business Ethics Quarterly, 12*(1), 19–32.
Moore, G. (2005a). Humanizing business: A modern virtue ethics approach. *Business Ethics Quarterly, 15*(2), 237–255.
Moore, G. (2005b). Corporate character: Modern virtue ethics and the virtuous corporation. *Business Ethics Quarterly, 15*(4), 659–685.
Moore, G. (2008). Re-imagining the morality of management: A modern virtue ethics approach. *Business Ethics Quarterly, 18*(4), 483–511.
Moore, G. (2012a). The virtue of governance, the governance of virtue. *Business Ethics Quarterly, 22*(2), 293–318.
Moore, G. (2012b). Virtue in business: Alliance boots and an empirical exploration of MacIntyre's conceptual framework. *Organization Studies., 33*(3), 363–387.
Moore, G. (2015). Corporate character, corporate virtues. *Business Ethics: A European Review, 24*(2), 99–114.
Moore, G. (2017). *Virtue at work: Ethics for individuals, managers and organisations*. Oxford University Press.
Nyssens, M. (Ed.). (2006). *Social enterprise*. Routledge.
Pearce, J. (2003). *Social enterprise in Anytown*. Calouste Gulbenkian.
Potter, B. (1904). *The co-operative movement in Great Britain*. Swan Sonnenschein & Co Limited.
Reeve, D., Brooke, C., & Williams, S. (2004). *Management case study biography of the co-operative bank*. University of Lincoln.
Ridley-Duff, R., & Bull, M. (2016). *Understanding social enterprise: theory and practice* (2nd ed.). Sage.
Spear, R., & Bidet, E. (2003). *The role of social enterprise in European labour markets*. European Research Network. https://emes.net/?id=203 (Accessed 22 March 2010).
Warren, R. C. (1996). The empty company: Morality and job security. *Personnel Review, 25*, 41–53.
Young, D. R. (1983). *If not for profit, for what? A behavioural theory of the nonprofit sector based on entrepreneurship*. Lexington Books.

CHAPTER 2

MacIntyre's Virtue

Introduction

This chapter elaborates on MacIntyre's views on the virtues by explaining what he defines as a practice and how this relates to the virtues. The role that practices plays within MacIntyre's larger body of work and what he defines as narrative and tradition are briefly discussed but the focus is primarily on his definition of a practice and how these can support individual achievement of the virtues. An essential aspect is the role of internal and external goods, where internal goods are linked to the practice and external goods are contingently attached, such as money, prestige and status. More specifically, it is the tension between internal and external goods and how they are ordered and prioritised in the institution which houses the practices. According to MacIntyre (2007), the institution is essential to the practice as it provides the structure for the practice to be developed and extended. However, MacIntyre asserts that institutions which do not prioritise practices, risk destroying the very practices they are designed to support, through corruption of the virtues and an excessive focus on external goods. Practices require the achievement of internal goods for the practitioners, which will be compromised when external goods are the focus. A commitment to the virtues is essential to the pursuit of practices; in particular, courage, justice and honesty are needed to ensure the practice is maintained, for without them it would not be a practice but a means to achieving external goods. MacIntyre

G. Hall, *Virtue and Social Enterprise*,
https://doi.org/10.1007/978-3-031-14027-3_2

argues that a focus on external goods is inimical to excellence, which is a necessary element of a practice. MacIntyre (2016) asserts that common goods are not simply a sum of individual goods but are prior to them; individual goods can only be achieved through the pursuit of common goods. Furthermore, MacIntyre (1999) argues that at various points in our lives we are vulnerable and dependent on others. For us to flourish we need the virtues that enable us to be independent practical reasoners and also those which enable us to realise our dependence on others (MacIntyre, 1999). Equally, we need to understand that others are dependent on us for their goods, through childhood, old age and illness. Such interdependence requires the virtues of 'just generosity' and 'acknowledged dependence' but for these to be achieved, it is necessary to participate in 'relationships of giving and receiving' (MacIntyre, 1999). MacIntyre suggests that networks of giving and receiving can be institutionalised within communities but, to be in good order they must be established through discussion and debate within the community. MacIntyre argues that common goods are those goods which benefit a whole community of practitioners and must be understood and prioritised by the practitioners for them to be able to attain individual goods such as personal achievement within a practice. The type of institutions which encourage and discourage practices is explored together with the influence of capitalistic and bureaucratic organisations in the pursuit of virtues in practice. MacIntyre argues that institutions that embody networks of giving and receiving and thus develop the virtues of just generosity and acknowledged dependence have an economic role, but they do not promote economic growth or the goals of consumer society and need protection from these outside forces. The role of cooperatives in the achievement of common goods is also considered. I conclude this chapter by arguing that capitalist institutions are not structured to support practices and internal goods because of a focus on external goods.

Practices

MacIntyre's definition of a practice was first fully articulated in his ground-breaking work *After Virtue* (published in 1981 with revised editions in 1984 and 2007[1]) and is used in a particular way, distinct from

[1] The 2nd edition added a postscript and the 3rd edition a prologue.

the regular use of the word practice. A practice for MacIntyre (2007) is essentially the context for understanding the virtues as they provide the environment in which virtues are demonstrated and defined. However, MacIntyre points out two caveats to his definition of practices; firstly, he emphasises that practices are not the only method of achieving the virtues, and that his definition of a practice serves to highlight part of a process towards the virtues. Practice forms the first of three stages which form the conceptual background to his conception of the virtues, with the narrative order to a human life and tradition being the latter two stages. The focus in this chapter is MacIntyre's practice, however his conception of the narrative order of a single human life and moral tradition are key elements to his views which are subsequent to a practice and presuppose the existence of the practice because it is the first of the three elements. The second caveat is his use of the word practice differs from the mainstream use. The Collins Dictionary (2018) defines practice as a customary way of doing something or the application of an idea or method. MacIntyre's definition of a practice requires human activity to be cooperatively created in which practitioners strive for excellence and in the process achieve internal goods particular to the practice, the result being that humans are able to extend their understanding of the goods and excellence associated with their practice.

For MacIntyre (2007), the aim of a practice is for its practitioners to determine the good and how it can be achieved, both in terms of ends to be achieved and the means, through cooperation with others engaged in the practice. MacIntyre's practice aims to articulate a view of virtue which encompasses individuals, communities of practitioners and the history of the practice. MacIntyre argues that bricklaying is not a practice according to his definition, whereas architecture is; kicking a ball is not a practice, whereas football is. His definition, therefore, relies on the complexity of the practice, the pursuit of excellence and the cooperation with others to ensure the virtues are pursued in the practice. Furthermore, attempts towards excellence in a given practice must be genuine to acquire the virtues. MacIntyre acknowledges that it is possible for practices to be evil according to his incomplete definition of virtue and practice. He supplements their definitions with the need to understand the telos of human life. Thus, MacIntyre argues that a complete definition of virtue and practice requires a commitment to virtue over the whole of one's lifetime, with an emphasis on the virtues. Even if it were possible to have evil practices, it would not be possible when considered in the context of the virtues and a whole life.

Internal and External Goods

MacIntyre (2007) goes on to explain the key terms in his definition of internal and external goods. External goods are those which are extrinsic to the practice such as the pursuit of money, wealth, prestige and status and so are not contingent on the practice for their achievement. He cites the example of a child playing chess who is initially induced to play the game in exchange for candy. Through playing the game of chess, he hopes that the child, in time, will discover the goods internal to the game. Internal goods might include the analytical skill, strategic ability and competitive spirit which are particular to the game of chess which provide the child with not only a reason to win beyond the candy incentive, but to excel at the game of chess in the manner in which the game dictates. MacIntyre deduces from this that there are two kinds of goods to be gained from the game of chess. Initially, the external good of the candy and then subsequently the internal goods which are highly specific to the game of chess. The external goods are not contingently attached to the game and can, therefore, be obtained through other means. External goods, such as money, prestige and status, are not therefore unique to the game of chess. The internal goods are exclusively attached to the practice, in this case, the game of chess. MacIntyre points out the meagreness of words in our vocabulary to describe such goods, which McMylor (1994) suggests, is why MacIntyre uses examples from games and portrait painting and argues that it is also because practices and goods do not take prominence in modern industrial capitalism where the focus tends to be on the rewards associated with profit and economic growth. MacIntyre resorts to using highly specific examples such as chess because internal goods can only be described in relation to a particular practice. Internal goods, according to MacIntyre, are only identifiable by those persons who have experience of engaging in the practice. It is through the pursuit of excellence that internal goods are realised by practitioners and since expectations of what ends can be achieved in a practice may be altered or completely modified as a consequence of engaging in the practice; it is from within the practice that these are realised.

To further elaborate on internal goods, MacIntyre (2007) uses the example of portrait painting where he suggests there are two kinds of internal goods. Firstly, the excellence in the product, both in terms of the final painting and in the performance of the painter. This creates an historical process which must consider all those who have developed and excelled in the practice up to that point. MacIntyre uses the example of the development of portrait painting in Western Europe from the Middle Ages to the eighteenth century to demonstrate the development of excellence within the practice of portrait painting in which depictions of the sitter developed around iconic and naturalistic depictions throughout the period. Furthermore, a willingness to accept the knowledge and achievements of all those who have gone before in a specific practice is essential. That is not to say that existing standards and achievements cannot be challenged. Indeed, a key aspect of striving for excellence in a practice is to extend the existing standards and to challenge them (Knight, 2007). Secondly, the sustained participation in the practice and attempting to push the boundaries of excellence within the practice create an understanding of what MacIntyre (2007) describes as the good of a particular sort of life. Since, MacIntyre argues, that to become an excellent painter requires a commitment by the painter to live one's life as a painter and therefore creates a certain kind of life in which the second type of internal good is achieved. MacIntyre later suggests that there are two ends to be achieved in the pursuit of a practice, firstly, the end state that is the objective of the practice, such as a portrait for a painter or a perfect crop for a farmer. Secondly, in pursuit of excellence, the individual strives to develop such qualities that optimise the practice and so for the portrait painter, it is to capture the features of the portrait sitter in a particular way. Furthermore, such aims and how they can be achieved or indeed, how they manifest in the end product, may be subject to modifications throughout the process. This is due to engagement in the practice being an evolving learning experience, which is driven by the pursuit of excellence, much like MacIntyre's example of the portrait painters throughout the sixteenth to the eighteenth centuries challenging the existing standards of excellence in terms of how a portrait should represent the sitter.

MacIntyre (2007) provides further elucidation of the essential difference between internal and external goods by stating that external goods are always someone's property, whereas when internal goods are obtained, the whole community of the practice gain too. MacIntyre uses the example of Turner painting seascapes in a new way, describing his achievement as enriching the entire associated community. Thus, both goods can be the outcome of competition according to MacIntyre, but there are no winners and losers as such when internal goods are achieved, whereas external goods are finite and therefore the more a person gains, the less there are for others. For MacIntyre, internal goods are only achieved when virtues are developed and exercised, without which, individuals would be unable to achieve those goods.

For MacIntyre (2007), without the virtues, the goods internal to practices are unavailable because, to access those goods requires a commitment to the virtues of justice, courage and honesty. To not fully commit to these virtues means that we do not fully commit to the practice. Thus, internal goods are not available and only external goods could be achieved as in MacIntyre's example of the child playing chess for candy. MacIntyre later finds goods of excellence as conducive to internal goods of a practice and goods of effectiveness as conducive to external goods which are characteristically pursued by institutions. He suggests that the qualities required in a person to pursue the external goods of power, money and prestige would require effectiveness in obtaining and utilising such goods and thus any goods obtained through these qualities would be called goods of effectiveness. To use MacIntyre's examples of a child playing chess and the portrait painter, the internal goods of excellence will not be achieved through cheating to win or by an efficient painting method. Internal goods of excellence require an adherence to other virtues, such as justice, for their existence and as such, will require a commitment to those virtues which will potentially be counter to the goods of effectiveness. MacIntyre (1988) explains that fairness and justice are required to excel because one must be able to judge and be judged on their achievement towards excellence in the practice. He argues that excellence cannot be broken down into a set of rules to follow, beyond established activities which characterise best practice so far. It is the unspecified ability to know how to extend such practice and know when to break with established practice to extend the excellence, that defines excellence in practice. To use MacIntyre's example of Turner's seascapes, breaking the 'rules' to create new excellence in seascape painting was not something that was taught to Turner, but more an understanding and a sustained commitment to the excellence of his practice which enabled such a development in his field. It would also require a knowledge of the history of painting and an understanding of the current practice of the community to be able to make that break.

Miller (1994) draws a distinction within MacIntyre's definition of a practice between 'self-contained' practices aimed at achieving the internal goods for the participant and 'purposive' practices which are intended to serve some social purpose beyond the practice. He suggests that MacIntyre's reference to games as practice relate to the first type and are usually straightforward in the distinction between internal and external goods. However, the latter, for example farming, is more complex because there is an external purpose which can be used to judge the practice (Miller, 1994). Miller, therefore, posits that the internal good is not simply internal to the practice and argues that in self-contained practices the critique can only come from within the practice, in accordance with MacIntyre's view, but purposive practices can be valued in relation to it end or outcome. MacIntyre regards all practices as self-contained according to Miller, even when the practice serves an obviously external purpose, citing MacIntyre who argues that excellence must be judged from within the practice, rather than considering a wider view. Miller argues that 'purposive practices' should be measured against how well it has served the external element of the practice, using external standards of justice. However, MacIntyre rejects Miller's argument stating that for virtue to exist, three types of good are necessary which relate to the practice, the individual and the community. An interdependence exists between the fishing crew which extends beyond the excellence in their craft to incorporate their families and wider community; MacIntyre (2016) refers to the three elements of crew, family and community as common goods in which individual ends are achieved through cooperation and the sustenance of their way of life. He argues that for a community to flourish it needs to support all practices, not in any hierarchy but ordered in such a way as to support a way of life (1988). MacIntyre is arguing that it is the activities and relationships of the community or fishing crew to support the practices, rather than reliance on external goods which is important. He argues that as soon as practices are valued for their external products, it creates a barrier to achieving the practice (1994). Ballard (2000) argues that MacIntyre's view of internal and external goods can be criticised where external outcomes can affect the practice. He cites farming and medicine as examples where the internal goods of a practice must be considered in relation to the social benefit of the product or service. However, he argues that MacIntyre successfully defends his position using the example of the two extreme fishing crews. Ballard asserts that MacIntyre is arguing that where work which could be a practice, is reduced to focusing on the external purpose, it can lead to a loss of internal goods for the individual and community. Ballard argues that MacIntyre could have given greater emphasis to the workers' cooperative tradition, given his negative view of the modern economic order and his views of the benefits of community. He points out systems such as Mondragon (a federation of workers' cooperatives) in which community structures encourage organisations which support practices and internal goods. Indeed, he argues that developing a cooperative model would be beneficial to MacIntyre's work since it encourages community action which can support internal goods. However, I would point out that MacIntyre (2016) does identify that cooperatives can support practices when citing examples such as Thorupstrand fishing village and the Monte Azul community where cooperatives support practices.

Common Goods

Essential to MacIntyre's view of a practice is the role that common goods play in the development of excellence in practice, both in terms of the adherence to historical developments in a practice and in the commitment to further developing excellence in practice. Indeed, Knight (1998) points out that MacIntyre described internal goods as goods of excellence, emphasising the importance of excellence in practice (1988). Common goods according to Knight (1998) are essential to a practice in that practitioners recognise that internal goods are not only achieved for themselves and for other practitioners in their practice, but also for wider society. Murphy (2003) elaborates on the centrality of common goods in practices, pointing out that common goods and practices occupy the same space. Murphy also points out an important difference between a common good and the public interest or public good, in that a public good is constituted by a prior knowledge of the individual good and thus public good serves the individual interest. For example, roads built to facilitate the ease of movement in society for people with cars. Whereas the common good has no prior individual good, it is not subordinated to any prior understanding of individual good and is not simply a means of achieving those preconceived ends through common pursuit (Murphy, 2003). In other words, there are no individual goods prior to the collective of individuals, only those goods which have been collectively pursued and understood by the group, towards a common end. Murphy refers to MacIntyre's fishing crew example in which the good for each member of the crew cannot be identified separately from the goods common to the crew members.

In MacIntyre's example of a fishing crew, he illustrates the difference between the external good of profit with the internal goods associated with a fishing crew. The example demonstrates the meaning of common goods in fishing dedicated to the practice of fishing within a community that has a shared understanding of the common goods to be achieved through excellence in cooperation. MacIntyre contrasts a fishing crew employed by an organisation with economic priorities to meet market demand for fish as profitably as possible, with a fishing crew which is not organised for primarily market reasons but instead, for the excellence to be achieved through fishing and being part of a fishing crew and wider fishing community. He asserts the skills and character qualities desirable for the economic crew focused only on profit will be developed towards achieving high profits. Commensurate with such values being held by both the organisation and the individual crew members, it is likely that where there are insufficient revenues to be gained from fishing, the result for both the owners of the organisation and the workers would be to find alternative sources of financial gain. Whereas, in the fishing crew dedicated to the excellence of fishing and being part of the crew, should an occasion arise where there is economic hardship associated with fishing, the crews are more likely to endure such hardships for as long as they are able. This is because of their dedication to both the craft of fishing and to the interrelated aspects of being a member of a fishing crew, such as the community and families reliant on fishing which override their desire for economic reward. Those individuals who have discovered the goods of excellence in fishing and being a fishing crew member will not be primarily motivated by external goods but will prize the internal goods of excellence in the fishing crew and of participating in the wider fishing community (MacIntyre, 1994).

The contrast between individual goods and common goods is clear in the fishing community example for the crews focused on economic rewards such as profits or high wages are pursuing individual goods, whereas the crew dedicated to excellence in fishing prioritise their being part of the crew. Such commitment according to MacIntyre also extends to families of the crew and to the fishing village community. Each worker's goals are common to all other workers in that they all aim to excel at fishing and a necessary element to that success is to behave cooperatively to ensure the safety and sustenance of the fishing community. MacIntyre is suggesting that it is not only the outcome of a practice that should be valued but also the social activities within a practice should be valued, provided they are carried out cooperatively and with excellence (Knight, 2007). Furthermore, Murphy (2003) points out the emphasis on cooperation in MacIntyre's definition of a practice in saying that there are two types of qualities necessary for achieving proficiency in a particular practice, which include the internal goods of the practice itself and the commitment to cooperation.

In addition, Macintyre (2016) argues that a political society is needed to understand and order the common goods of society. He argues that a political society involves those people who have common concerns such as family, school and workplace which is a different definition from the bureaucratic state of government in which elected members make decisions on society's behalf. MacIntyre claims that as soon as a group of individuals identify with their common goods and what is needed for them and their families to flourish, they begin to concern themselves with politics. He suggests that decisions about common goods should be carried out in shared deliberation independent of individual interests of the participants but with an assumption that all members largely agree on the goods that are at stake in their decision-making. Thus, it is not bargaining between competing interests but rather, bargaining may be necessary to determine the priorities of the community. Furthermore, such deliberations must be conducted to ensure that each individual who has an interest in the common good is given a voice and is not threatened or influenced in any way. MacIntyre includes schools, trade unions and community organisations as being participants in the political decision-making in society; he argues that concern for the common good can give rise to political actions through such organisations, when individuals appreciate that their individual goods are indelibly linked to common goods. MacIntyre's description of the necessary elements of a politics of making and sustaining local communities can be summarised as:

- Shared deliberation governed by standards independent of individual desires and interests of those involved
- Agreement on the goods at stake in the interests of local community
- Largely a shared conception of how goods should be achieved
- Every relevant voice is heard
- Every argument given due weight, not because of power or influence.

(Paraphrased from MacIntyre, 2016)

MacIntyre cites the example of Thorupstrand in which a community of fishing crews, faced with the introduction of individual fishing quotas which could have destroyed their fishing community with privatisation of the industry, decided to retain their shared community reliant on fishing by establishing a cooperative company. The cooperative relied on the virtues of those involved in the cooperative and the elements of political association described, for its ability to compete in the market system created by the fishing quotas (MacIntyre, 2016). They demonstrated shared deliberation, agreement on the goods at stake and how they should be achieved through a cooperative approach to ensure democratic decision-making.

Virtues

MacIntyre (2007) draws on Homer, Aristotle, the New Testament, Benjamin Franklin and Jane Austen to create a conception of virtue, but determines that there is no agreed definition of the concept of virtue. However, he argues that they all follow a process in determining their definition of virtues by using excellence in practical reasoning (Lutz, 2012). MacIntyre (2007) defines a virtue as a human quality which is acquired and developed through its exercise, which enables the achievement of internal goods through practice. This is not a complete definition according to MacIntyre, but it does serve to highlight the relationship between virtue and practice because there are key virtues necessary to a true engagement in a practice which cannot be impersonated or avoided. MacIntyre claims that there must be some type of relationship between all practitioners in a practice. He argues that the virtues are goods within a practice which form part of the relationships between practitioners, through their shared purpose and standards of achievement which relate to the practice. MacIntyre gives the example of a professor who gives a grade for a paper to a student based on their attractiveness, whereas the other papers are graded based on the mark the paper deserves. In effect, the professor is creating a different relationship with the attractive student to the other class members. Justice requires that people are treated according to merit or desert, based on a set of standards. Thus, MacIntyre argues that justice is necessary in a practice to ensure that all involved are treated in a uniform manner and not using some standard other than those of the practice. Clearly, trust and honesty link to justice or else the understanding and expectation of practitioners would be eroded. Those involved in a practice need to be able to rely on there being no differences in relationships, or how they are treated, other than those determined by the shared standards and purpose of the practice (Taylor, 2005).

MacIntyre (2007) cites courage as a virtue in practice because it is a crucial element to caring about individuals and communities. He argues that it is not possible to say you care for a particular individual, without being willing to risk harm to yourself. He points out that it is possible to care but not be able to risk harm to yourself, but that would require the individual to acknowledge their own cowardice. For the most part, those who say they are concerned but are unwilling to put themselves at risk of harm, cast doubt on the genuineness of their concern. MacIntyre argues that it is, therefore, essential to include the virtues of justice, courage and honesty in regard to the excellence of a practice. To do anything other would be a means to achieving only external goods, as in the example of the child obtaining candy through playing chess. MacIntyre acknowledges that where there are virtues there may also be vices, but those who are vicious, rely on the virtue of others to enable them to flourish in their activity and thereby deny themselves the possibility to obtain the internal goods associated with that practice. Furthermore, MacIntyre argues that virtues can flourish in different types of societies but cannot flourish in societies which do not value the virtues.

MacIntyre points out that what is distinctive of a practice is how the internal goods of a particular practice are 'transformed and enriched' through the development and progression by those involved in the practice. In other words, a practice is something far more than a set of skills which can be learned and carried out following careful learning and instruction. It is partly related to how such skills become so much more when those skills are developed through excellence and are distinctive to a practice. The attainment of internal goods requires a far more dedicated commitment to the practice which requires respect and understanding of its history and a commitment to its ongoing development. A practice requires an appreciation of those who have preceded in the practice as well as current practitioners and a willingness to learn from the existing standards of the practice which have been developed to their current standard by those who have gone before. To engage with the existing traditions and to accept the authority of the history of the practice require the virtues of courage, justice and truthfulness.

MacIntyre (1999) develops the virtues required for common goods, with acknowledged dependence and just generosity. He argues that we use our independent practical reasoning to pursue our own goods, but for its full exercise, an understanding of acknowledged dependence is also necessary. Acknowledged dependence requires an appreciation that throughout our lives we are dependent on others for our goods. This could be during childhood, old age or illness or an accident which has caused temporary or permanent disability to the extent that we are unable to pursue our own goods without the assistance of others (MacIntyre, 1999). Equally, we are responsible for the care of others throughout our lives and helping them to achieve their goods because they are unable to pursue them for themselves because of age or illness. An acknowledgement of our interdependence throughout our lives is necessary to understanding the common goods we share and to develop networks of giving and receiving in which goods are genuinely common because they belong to everyone (MacIntyre, 1999). For this type of virtue to be achieved, MacIntyre suggests that 'just generosity' is needed to appreciate the intricate relationships of family and community; such virtues require us to act in a just and generous manner and the development of which will develop the ability to have relationships of uncalculated giving and receiving. Furthermore, acknowledged dependence makes clear that common goods are prior to individual goods since we can only achieve our goods when we acknowledge our interdependence and know that we rely on each other and therefore must consider the goods of others. MacIntyre elaborates on the types of environment in which acknowledged dependence can be developed and argues that institutions have such potential where networks of giving and receiving are present. However, such an institution would need to have a form of deliberation which included all members and just generosity to ensure justice for all. He observes that neither the state nor family are equipped to provide such a network of giving and receiving but refers to the 'intermediate area' between these in which communities and institutions can develop and maintain the virtue of just generosity. It is within such institutions and communities that a shared understanding of the common good is an integral part of their activities (MacIntyre, 1999). For such institutions or communities to be in good order, according to MacIntyre, they would need to engage in shared deliberation regarding their own standards and judgements and ensure that such discussions informed the development of the institution or community.

Institutions

Practices, according to MacIntyre, should be distinguished from institutions. The institution provides the support for the practice by obtaining the external goods such as money and other material goods for the practice to survive. However, he suggests that practices can be vulnerable to certain institutions if the external goods pursued by the institution are allowed to interfere with the practice, external goods such as money, power and status (MacIntyre, 1994). He argues that external goods are necessary and in relation to practices and he suggests that practices cannot be sustained without the institution. However, due to the nature of external goods being such things as money, power and status, the practice can become vulnerable to an excessive focus on external goods in the institution, at the expense of the internal goods of the practice. Indeed, MacIntyre states that such is the intimacy of the relationship of practices to institutions that they form a 'single causal order' whereby practices are vulnerable to the actions of the institution. Essentially, according to MacIntyre (2007), the institution is focused on acquisitiveness and competition, which creates risk for the common goods associated with the practice. Again, he points out the need for the virtues of justice, courage and honesty in ensuring that practices do not become secondary to the institutional drive for external goods or their corrupting power which can subvert a practice to ensure that it provides the means to power, prestige and money, rather than focus on internal goods of excellence. Knight (2007) interprets MacIntyre as saying such is the case under capitalism whereby corporations and the state systematically ensure that external goods are pursued, to the exclusion of goods of excellence as defined by MacIntyre.

MacIntyre (2007) further suggests that certain types of institutions may have the characteristics of a practice if they are involved in creating and sustaining a community. The learning of virtues and the ability to exercise those virtues rely on how communities are made and sustained, and inherent to such a community is its institutional form. Such human communities or institutions play a key role in determining whether its citizens learn to exercise the virtues and impacts on the practices within such communities; for practices require the virtues for their existence. However, the role of virtues and their predominance depends on the social and political context in which these forms of institutions operate.

For MacIntyre, it is communities which provide the structures for practices to flourish through institutions which establish and enforce the existing standards expected in the practice. However, MacIntyre views modern society as being governed by liberal individualism which focuses on an individual's right to pursue their own interest. The key difference between the liberal individualism of modernity and the ancient traditions, according to MacIntyre, is the understanding of what creates the good life; liberal individualism views the role of political institutions as being morally neutral and exists simply to maintain law and order to enable individuals to pursue their own interpretation of the good life. Whereas according to MacIntyre, the ancient view holds the virtues as central to the political community and requires the virtues to be both exercised and taught to the next generation to ensure the continued sustainability of the institution. The distinction between the two approaches of liberal individualism and the ancient view is sharp, particularly given that virtues in MacIntyre's account are so central. For MacIntyre, the social and political institutions in society have a key role in determining the extent to which virtues are embodied in their practices. Social institutions may either encourage and develop the virtues or endanger them and according to MacIntyre, the modern state, with its liberal individualist standpoint is not fit to provide a moral education of virtue to any community. MacIntyre suggests that a society within modern commercialism which lacks the virtues would only have the external goods of power, money and status and would fail to recognise the internal goods associated with practice. The lack of virtues in modern economic or commercial society in which the virtues and internal goods are secondary to the external goods of the institution is the foundation of this book. The virtues are necessary to achieve internal goods but may be a hindrance in achieving external goods according to MacIntyre, who argues that virtues such as truthfulness, justice and courage may prevent us from becoming wealthy and powerful. MacIntyre acknowledges that external goods are still goods and ideally people would like to achieve both internal and external goods. However, given that internal goods can hinder the acquisition of external goods, MacIntyre argues that in a society where external goods are dominant it could result in a decline in the virtues. It is argued here that modern capitalist enterprise supports the prioritising of external goods and thus, an erosion of the virtues associated with internal goods. It is clear that MacIntyre views the type of institution and its priorities as fundamental to the achievement of individual and common goods.

In particular, the workplace can present the most difficult challenges in developing the virtues and a commitment to common goods in the community (MacIntyre, 2016). For MacIntyre, there are two distinct ways of evaluating a workplace; one is through economic or market logic of value and the other is independent of such issues and is reliant on the values of individual and common goods. He argues that the institutional form which houses the practice is critical to ensuring the integrity of the virtues because some institutions will encourage them, whilst others may endanger them (MacIntyre, 2007).

MacIntyre, in support of his view that politics can be part of society through communities and not only performed by the modern state and its bureaucratic institutions, cites examples of individuals combining to achieve the common goods of family, workplace, school and society more generally; theirs are stories of political and economic concern despite not being derived from the state or market forces. MacIntyre (2016) points out that institutions which provide for practices which achieve common goods are often cooperatives. MacIntyre recounts the story of Thorupstrand in which a fishing community with a significant history in shared fishing created a cooperative when faced with legislation to privatise fishing quotas to individual boats. The cooperative company made up of twenty families purchased a common pool of quotas, with decisions being democratically based on one member–one vote with responsibility for maintaining the practice of share fishing being jointly assumed by all the families. The practice of share fishing was already a cooperative activity through maintaining the boats and the supporting structure of the community which relied on fishing and with all earnings and losses being shared proportionately amongst the crew. However, the purchase of a common pool of quotas gave rise to a more formal structure to the cooperation. MacIntyre determines the virtues that were essential to its success as the qualities of mind and character by those involved in the new cooperative; prudence, justice, courage and temperateness as essential virtues, without which the venture would likely have failed. He also remarks on the close association between family and the workplace and suggests that there is understanding of the common good and how they are related across the different aspects of the community life (MacIntyre, 2016). The fishing community of Thorupstrand which attempted to avoid the individualism inherent in the type of fishing quotas being introduced, by establishing a cooperative which served the community. MacIntyre argues that the community survived and flourished because of its prudence in its economic approach to the market and to the state; justice in their management of the cooperative and courage in their risk taking and also restraint where there were temptations from the individual financial rewards possible from the quota opportunity. MacIntyre also cites Monte Azul as an example of a local community which has established a politics of the common good through institutions and organisations for its promotion. According to MacIntyre, Monte Azul, a slum in Brazil, epitomised the inequalities inherent to capitalism in terms of wealth and poverty. The cooperative initiatives improved sanitation, education and health care through campaigning but MacIntyre focuses on the characteristics of the organisations which were instrumental in these changes. He identifies that groups of campaigners met regularly to identify their common goods and how they could be achieved. MacIntyre argues that such groups applied the same virtues as the fishing village of Thorupstrand of political prudence, justice, courage and temperateness in successfully improving the lives of the community of Monte Azul. MacIntyre (2016) points out that flourishing could only be achieved through the commitment of the participants in the shared deliberation to determine their common goods and equity in decision-making. He also argues that such examples are contrary to the economic model prevalent in capitalist societies whereby individuals seek to maximise their preferences without regard for their community or others. Such individuals, using practical reasoning, would use competitive advantage to maximise their satisfaction, rather than shared deliberation to determine the common goods. MacIntyre cites Elinor Ostrom as demonstrating the falsity that all individuals are preference maximisers by using numerous examples of successful communal management at both local and regional levels.

Capitalistic and Bureaucratic Institutions

It is also clear from MacIntyre's (2007) writing that for virtues to flourish, practices need to be supported by institutions which nurture and encourage a respect for the history of the practice and the pursuit of excellence. The ends of a practice are embodied in the virtues according to MacIntyre and manifest in both the product and the practitioner. However, the extent to which practices can achieve their ends is largely governed by the type of institution to which it is connected (MacIntyre, 2007). MacIntyre is highly critical of capitalistic and bureaucratic institutions since these are structured to ensure that the ends of the organisation take precedence over the individuals' ability to pursue practices through defining the work of those employed by the institution; the ends being the external goods of wealth, or in the case of state-run institutions, public goods such as law and order. According to MacIntyre, all bureaucratic institutions are organised for effectiveness using costs and benefits. In particular, it is the function of management and managers to ensure that activity is directed towards the institutional ends and therefore ensure that all workers' activity is focused accordingly. MacIntyre makes a distinction between two types of work or activity in which one type is self-directed by the worker and the other is determined by managers. The former involves a mode of practice according to MacIntyre (2016) whereby workers can identify and pursue the ends they believe to be worthwhile and thereby hold themselves to a set of self-determined standards of excellence, whereas the latter is an activity in which ends are imposed by managers and therefore not the ends of the worker. MacIntyre (1988) points out that it is not possible to reduce a practice to a set of rules, without providing for the possibility of extending the boundaries of the practice. Indeed, Knight (2007) points out that progress in practices is only achieved through such freedom. However, MacIntyre's criticism of management and its corrupting influence on practices have not gone unchallenged; Brewer (1997) argues that business can be a complex, cooperative social activity in accordance with MacIntyre's definition and management operate within a socially established field. She argues that management operate in a complex environment which is not only economic, but also social, political and moral. She cites Bowie (1991) and Frank (1988) and argues that self-interest is not the only incentive for management, instead cooperation is also involved. Furthermore, Brewer argues that even if management were operating on purely economic motives, cooperation would still be used because it can benefit self-interest. MacIntyre's (2007) view is that the modern economic order is not conducive to the virtues, particularly individualism and acquisitiveness which have been given a central place in society. Sinnicks (2018) points out that management is not inherently immoral suggesting that many authors have demonstrated management as mostly amoral, some immoral and some moral. Dawson and Bartholomew (2003) found themselves relating business more to a practice than management, on the basis that those involved in directing and influencing the productive process and products needed to have in-depth understanding and knowledge of how their product or service contributes to the common good. Beabout (2013) has addressed MacIntyre's criticism at length and asserts that it is possible for management to be a domain-relative practice in which it has standards of excellence internal to managerial tasks, whilst being related to a different practice within the same institutional setting. However, the key issue with management as a practice is with management within capitalist institutions, which are largely driven by the profit-maximising motive. The scholars cited who criticise MacIntyre's denial of management as a practice are attempting to do so from a business context, which falls within the capitalist system which MacIntyre is so critical of because of the individualism and acquisitiveness associated with it. However, MacIntyre (2016), in his more recent work, uses an example from business of the Japanese automobile industry to demonstrate that workers in the factory can achieve excellence in car production. He argues that devolving responsibility for a car's production from management to a team of workers enables them to achieve excellence in their ability to make cars and produce excellent cars. The team working enables the workers to engage in shared deliberation and decision-making towards a common good, which is the production of an excellent car using standards that are self-imposed, rather than from management. However, I argue that despite the autonomy allowed for the car production workers over how the car is produced, the influence of profit maximising in a capitalist system will still prevent such workers achieving excellence for themselves and their product if the ends that the company wants to achieve are profit maximisation. MacIntyre points out that the Japanese workers can direct their own work and therefore make it their own. However, MacIntyre argues that workplaces are often not the environment where common goods can be achieved and more often organised in the most cost-effective way to achieve maximum productivity and profit. MacIntyre suggests that this occurs in a typical capitalist organisation when describing the worker as serving the ends of the company for the sake of a wage and views effectiveness as dominating over excellence (Beadle, 2002).

MacIntyre's (2007) view of capitalism takes into consideration its historical context in that he determines the change in how production moved away from the household to servicing capital demands, which fundamentally altered the understanding of how to achieve goods for individuals, family and community. He refers to the transformation of the social context from family and community-based work to the externalising of livelihoods and dependence on the market in which we now live and the relentless dominance of the markets in critiquing the loss of practice and virtue from a central role in society. For the owners of capital are driven by pleonexia or acquisitiveness according to MacIntyre (2016) in the pursuit of wealth, whilst workers are simply the means to achieving such ends. Thus, workers' ends are external in the form of salary or financial reward, internal goods are not available to workers in such a means-end relationship and correspondingly, neither are practices (MacIntyre, 2007). This has resulted in the marginalisation of practices in favour of the endless production lines which are inimical to the achievement of internal goods. MacIntyre (2016) argues that a commitment to common goods is essential to achieving individual goods and, in an institutional context, there should be a determination to encourage practices in which common goods can be achieved. MacIntyre is critical of Adam Smith, pointing out that Smith had omitted to recognise the relationship between common goods and individual goods in his account of economic trade. Smith refers to a general good as the good of the majority in the long run, which can be achieved through each individual pursuing their own interests. Whereas MacIntyre (2016) argues that cooperation in achieving common goods is essential to be able to obtain individual goods, because common goods are prior to individual goods. According to MacIntyre, there can be no conception of individual goods, without first understanding and committing to common goods.

According to MacIntyre (2016), a key element to the economic development of capitalism was explained by Marx in his account of how individuals viewed themselves and their social relationships. For those whose labour is for hire to view themselves as anything other than a commodity within a system which attributes surplus value of their labour to the owners of the means of production, workers needed to believe they were pursuing their own interests through contractual agreements, rather than being simply commodities for hire. Individual pursuit of desires was to become the acceptable norm which are sharply contrasted with MacIntyre's views of the common good. The appropriated surplus value is used to further the productivity that is needed in a capitalist system through profits which are invested in enterprises for economic growth. MacIntyre suggests that to have any conception of the cultural and social changes, it is necessary to understand Marx's description of capitalism and its destructive nature. MacIntyre sees the Thomistic and Marxist influence as creating an opportunity to create institutions that encourage and develop practices through which common goods and consequently individual goods can be achieved. However, such organisations are in the form of a cooperative organisation and as such may suffer because they challenge the dominance of a culture which is rooted in individualism. MacIntyre does not detail other types of organisations other than cooperatives which support common goods through practice, but I argue that other types of enterprise exist which support common and individual goods, in particular radical social enterprises.

MacIntyre takes issue with what he refers to as the modern economic order in relation to our understanding and application of the virtues. Blackledge (2009) points out that MacIntyre views the free market as a means of thwarting the collective deliberation by individuals on common goods and indeed that free-market institutions are damaging to the virtues. MacIntyre refers to the central place that market values have in our society and the focus on individualism and acquisitiveness which are encouraged within such a society, at the expense of the tradition of the virtues. Despite recognising that productive work can contribute to the common good and excellence in his discussion of the Japanese automobile industry (MacIntyre, 2016), MacIntyre points out that profit remains a key factor. He suggests that organisations which are struggling to be profitable can be driven to the production of harmful goods or creating methods of production which increase profitability but harm excellence in practice (MacIntyre, 2016).

The capitalist system of a market economy when efficiency has primacy over excellence is detrimental to practices when workers are only able to achieve the external good of a wage. MacIntyre argues that capitalism is driven by the external goods of money, status and wealth which are inimical to excellence.

Conclusion

MacIntyre's work on virtues establishes a coherent grounding for understanding the role of the virtues and how they may be achieved. He makes clear the relationship and tension between internal and external goods and how, despite external goods still being goods, they can have a corrupting influence on the pursuit of the internal goods associated with a practice. Furthermore, the role of common goods is shown to be inexorably linked to practices in that they are prior to individual goods; without an understanding and pursuit of the common goods, it is not possible to realise individual goods. It is as independent practical reasoners that we learn to cooperate with others to achieve our common goods but acknowledged dependence and just generosity are essential virtues to developing our common goods. Fundamental to the practice is the institution and how it supports the practice which it houses. The definition of what constitutes a practice and the type of institution which supports a practice is contentious with academics suggesting a broader range of practices than MacIntyre, particularly the ability of the workplace to be conducive to practices. The next chapter will explore business as a mode of institution and whether it could be deemed to encourage and support practices. I argue that institutions are unwilling and unable to pursue practices which support internal goods when the economic market supports individualism and profit maximisation. Indeed, it is organisations outside of the market system which are not based on capital ownership which are best suited to MacIntyre's views.

References

Ballard, B. (2000). *Understanding MacIntyre*. University Press of America.

Beabout, G. R. (2013). *The character of the manager*. Palgrave Macmillan.

Beadle, R. (2002). The misappropriation of MacIntyre. *Reason in Practice, 2*, 45–54.

Blackledge, P. (2009). Alasdair MacIntyre: Social practices marxism and ethical anti-capitalism. *Political Studies, 57*(4), 866–884. https://doi.org/10.1111/j.1467-9248.2008.00770.x

Bowie, N. (1991). Challenging the egoistic paradigm. *Business Ethics Quarterly, 1*(1), 1–21.

Brewer, K. B. (1997). Management as practice: A response to Alasdair MacIntyre. *Journal of Business Ethics, 16*(8), 825–833.

Dawson, D., & Bartholomew, C. (2003). Virtues, managers and business people: Finding a place for MacIntyre in a business context. *Journal of Business Ethics, 48*, 127–138.

Frank, R. (1988). *Passions within reason: The strategic role of the emotions*. W.W. Norton & Company.

Knight, K. (1998). *The MacIntyre reader*. Polity Press.

Knight, K. (2007). *Aristotelian philosophy: Ethics and politics from Aristotle to MacIntyre*. Polity Press.

Lutz, C. S. (2012). *Reading Alasdair MacIntyre's after virtue*. Continuum International Publishing Group.

MacIntyre, A. (1988). *Whose justice? Which rationality?* Duckworth & Co.

MacIntyre, A. (1994). A partial response to my critics. In J. Horton & S. Mendus (Eds.), *After MacIntyre* (pp. 283–304). Polity Press.

MacIntyre, A. (1999). *Dependent rational animals: Why human beings need the virtues*. Carus Publishing Company.
MacIntyre, A. (2007). *After virtue* (3rd ed.). University of Notre Dame Press.
MacIntyre, A. (2016). *Ethics in the conflicts of modernity: An essay on desire, practical reasoning and narrative*. Cambridge University Press.
McMylor, P. (1994). *Alasdair MacIntyre critic of modernity*. Routledge.
Miller, D. (1994). Virtues, practices and justice. In J. Horton & S. Mendus (Eds.), *After MacIntyre* (pp. 283–304). Polity Press.
Murphy, M. C. (Ed.). (2003). *Alasdair MacIntyre*. Cambridge University Press.
Sinnicks, M. (2018). Leadership after virtue: MacIntyre's critique of management reconsidered. *Journal of Business Ethics, 147*, 735–746.
Taylor, J. (2005). *Virtue ethics "in practice": An exposition on and defence of Alasdair MacIntyre's theory of practices in after virtue*. Dallas Baptist University. http://www.dbu.edu (Accessed 2 June 2019).

CHAPTER 3

MacIntyre's Virtues and Capitalism

Introduction

The focus of this chapter is to explore the validity and role of MacIntyre's virtues to capitalist business. Indeed, whether or not MacIntyre's work on virtues can be applied to business and in what context; can business be deemed a practice or practice embodying institutions, or are they inimical to practices and the pursuit of excellence? Keat (2008) observes that central to MacIntyre in *After Virtue* (2007) is that a practice is incompatible with capitalism. That businesses operate in the capitalist free market system is a fundamental issue because of the pursuit of profit maximisation and individualism on which the system thrives, is potentially in conflict with MacIntyre's focus on internal goods and virtue through excellence, as explored in the previous chapter. It is argued that capitalist organisations are controlled by the owners of capital who use effectiveness—rather than excellence—to achieve their ends of capital accumulation. Indeed, Beadle (2002) points out that MacIntyre views business organisations as being based on effectiveness, which is achieved through power, rather than virtue. This is contrary to MacIntyre's view, articulated in the previous chapter, of an organisation which strives for excellence in practice through shared deliberation and a mutual understanding of common goods and how they can be achieved. Furthermore, MacIntyre argues that capitalism does not take a supporting role in society, but rather its nature is to become dominant (Beadle, 2002). However, Moore (2002)

G. Hall, *Virtue and Social Enterprise*,
https://doi.org/10.1007/978-3-031-14027-3_3

argues that business can fit within MacIntyre's definition of a practice because they engage in cooperative human activities, of a complex and coherent nature. Moore acknowledges that MacIntyre views capitalism as having an excessive focus on external goods but argues that it does not preclude business as a practice. However, I argue that it is not possible for all businesses to be a practice precisely because of the institutional arrangement which provides for the practice. In capitalist organisations, the primary motivation of profit is determined and guided by the owners of capital and the institutional structure ensures that wealth accumulation is the focus for the organisation. For MacIntyre, there is a strict hierarchy in which external goods are subordinated to internal goods; there can be no balancing of priorities between external goods such as wealth and the internal goods of practices. MacIntyre claims that effectiveness is achieved by the institutional control of labour, in particular through the division of labour (Moore, 2002). Furthermore, Moore (2002) acknowledges in attempting to define business as a practice, that business is frequently valued through its external goods, which is clearly at odds with MacIntyre and the importance of internal goods in practice. However, Moore (2005a) sees no fundamental problem with aligning business with practice and corporation with institution and believes that MacIntyre's understanding of the corrupting powers of institutions and the importance of virtues to sustain the practice indicate that corporate business epitomises such a challenge. Moore (2015) argues that because external goods are deemed to be genuine goods by MacIntyre, this means that business can withstand MacIntyre's critique of capitalism. Moore (2005b) argues that if business organisations were committed to the virtues, then it would be possible to create virtuous organisations, which could support practices. He argues that the organisation must always observe its founding purpose of the practice and it is the responsibility of the practitioners to ensure that the organisation retains this focus (Moore, 2002). But for the practitioners to be able to do this, they would need to hold the power of decision-making in the organisation to ensure such focus was retained. In capitalist organisations, the power to make decisions is held by the owners of capital, who are not always the practitioners particularly in large corporations. Without an organisational structure which enables the shared deliberation of practitioners to develop virtues and determine their common and individual goods, there is no guarantee that external goods will not become the focus. I contend that without a fundamental change to the priority of capital and the decision-making powers in the institution to a strict ordering of common goods and internal goods as dominant over external goods, it is not possible to interpret MacIntyre as being supportive of capitalist businesses. Moore argues that the creation of a virtuous business organisation could, if it were to gain general application, create widespread opportunity for MacIntyre's modern virtue theory to flourish because it would positively influence capitalism. However, a key feature of capitalism is its dominance and control over society according to MacIntyre, rather than playing a supportive role in society (Beadle, 2002). Beadle (2002) argues that MacIntyre considers capitalist business as intrinsically ruthless and precludes the achievement of individual virtue. It is argued here that it is not possible to reform capitalism in the way Moore intends. I agree with MacIntyre's pessimistic view of capitalism and its inability to become virtuous. However, it will be later argued that alternative organisations exist outside of the capitalist system which do conform to MacIntyre's views. In particular, the radical form of social enterprise will be analysed to assess its compatibility with MacIntyre.

Keat (2008) elaborates on types of capitalism and asserts that it is possible for a particular type of capitalism to be conducive to practices because of its institutional structure allowing for cooperation and providing for internal goods to be achieved. MacIntyre's view of practice requires cooperation between practitioners and the ability of practitioners to pursue internal goods, as discussed in Chapter 2. Equally, Keat argues, certain types of capitalism are antithetical to a practice type of production. Keat claims that institutions embodied in different types of capitalism vary in their ability to resist the acquisitiveness and short-termism associated with the excessive pursuit of external goods, at the expense of internal goods.

Keat (2008) argues that MacIntyre views external goods as still goods, because they are necessary for the institution, which in turn, is necessary for the development of practices. Therefore, the problem with capitalism, for MacIntyre, must be related to the nature of capitalist institutions and their influence on practice, rather than the existence of external goods. According to Keat, MacIntyre, when referring to the money motivated fishing crew in his example, is relying on the reader's assumption that he is referring to the liberal form of capitalism, rather than other types of capitalism found in countries such as Germany or Japan. Keat (2008) uses Hall and Soskice's work (2001) on the varieties of capitalism to identify the UK and USA as having a Liberal Market Economy (LME). Such economies tend towards share ownership by large pension funds that are sensitive to short-term profit changes and governance structures which are bureaucratic and hierarchical and lacking in devolved decision-making. However, an important observation by Keat is that his varieties of capitalism analysis only consider the extent to which institutions focus on the external goods of profit and financial reward, rather than a focus on how committed they are to internal goods and practice. This is an important distinction in this book as it will be demonstrated that institutions which prioritise common goods and subsequently internal goods and subordinate external goods are more likely to be practice conducive institutions. Whereas, liberal capitalist institutions focus on external goods, albeit to greater or lesser extents, and consider internal goods as a secondary issue, if at all. The purpose of this chapter is to demonstrate that liberal capitalism, which focus on external goods of profit, wealth and prestige, using an individualist culture which focuses on individual gain above community, are unsuitable for creating practice focused institutions in accordance with MacIntyre.

Moore attempts to demonstrate the ability of business to be a practice and for capitalist companies to be institutions in accordance with MacIntyre. Moore alludes to an ideal type of business organisation (2005a, 2005b, 2008, 2012a, 2012b, 2015) which suggests that reforms would be needed before the current capitalist system could be suitable for the application of MacIntyre's virtue theory. Moore (2002) focuses on business in his use of MacIntyre's theory and the distinction between practice and institution in the development of virtue. He has theorised that business can be defined as a 'practice' and the corporation as an 'institution' according to MacIntyre's definition; with the aim of creating a means for business ethics to be conceptualised using virtue ethics theory. In the application of MacIntyre's work, Moore (2005b) later develops a set of virtuous corporate characteristics which, if in place in an organisation, create the ideally virtuous corporation. It is Moore's contention that the virtuous corporation requires the cardinal virtues such as wisdom, temperance and justice to withstand the corrupting powers of non-virtuous institutions with which it is required to associate, such as competitors, suppliers and customers. For business to be fully 'humanised', according to Moore, it is essential that both management and the corporation as the institution recognise the need to be virtuous.

The virtuous corporation, according to Moore (2012b) would have a 'good purpose' and the institution would be founded on that purpose and ensure its achievement through a commitment to it as a practice.

External goods would only be pursued for the purposes of sustaining and developing the practice. Moore suggests that a good purpose can be determined by how well the practice, which is at the core of the organisation, contributes to the good of the community. He argues that to ensure such an outcome requires an ongoing debate within the organisation and with the community, citing MacIntyre's shared deliberation as essential. It is argued in this chapter, in accordance with Moore that liberal capitalism is not structured to enable such a virtuous organisation. Moore acknowledges that in an environment where external goods are preferred over internal goods, it would be difficult for the virtuous organisation to survive. However, he suggests an environment where businesses recognise their responsibility in relation to the virtues and an environment which incorporates a change in the market, regulatory systems, role of labour and capital within business, would enable virtuous organisations to exist (Moore, 2015).

Business as Practice; Corporation as Institution

As mentioned earlier, Moore (2002) argues that business can be defined as a practice and the corporation as an institution. MacIntyre views internal goods as being the key element in a practice and ultimately of the virtues, as explored in Chapter 2. Internal goods, per MacIntyre, rely on acceptance that there is an existing body and standard of knowledge within a practice which needs to be learned, and as a result of such learning it becomes possible to extend that knowledge to attain excellence in the practice. Thus, internal goods are communal within the practice because those attempting to learn and excel will do so from the existing body of expertise and the further development in the field through their contribution (MacIntyre, 2007). MacIntyre is not averse to competition, but only within the practice where such achievement benefits all practitioners, rather than individuals only. Virtue is achieved through the acquisition of excellence, through his definition of a practice. Internal goods, which are directly linked to the achievements in a practice, are contrasted with external goods which are contingently linked to the practice, such as fame, power, status or money. MacIntyre (2007) points out an important difference between the goods in that external goods are always belonging to someone, unlike internal goods which tend to also have a wider benefit beyond the individual, through the community involved in the practice. The institution sustains the practice according to

MacIntyre, for example, a hospital is the institution which serves the practice of medicine. Institutions are concerned with external goods according to MacIntyre, which is necessary to the extent that the practice needs to be sustained; external goods provide the practical means to support the practice and create an environment for the practices to be pursued. However, MacIntyre acknowledges that not all institutions are supportive of practices and that without the virtues, institutions are likely to be corrupted through an excessive focus on external goods. In the previous chapter, it was identified that MacIntyre views internal goods associated with practice should be prioritised by an institution for it to conform with his work. Moore (2002) argues that if a business institution were to become virtuous, it would be able to withstand the acquisitiveness associated with the pursuit of external goods. Therefore, focusing more on the internal goods of the practice and only on external goods to the extent that they support the practice. However, for business organisations to be able to do this, it would require a different understanding of its purpose, such that external goods of profit were only pursued as the means to the end of securing internal goods. My view is that central to MacIntyre is a commitment to the internal goods of practice and only those external goods necessary for the sustenance of the practice should be pursued, as explained in the previous chapter. MacIntyre requires that external goods are subordinated to internal goods. Moore (2002) acknowledges that his virtuous organisation theory is a theory which is not reflected in capitalist business currently but holds the belief that if they were to become widespread, they would have a positive impact on capitalism. The liberal capitalist corporation is committed to the pursuit of profit and wealth and is structured so that the owners of capital, in the form of shareholders receive an external good in the form of dividends and share value. In the previous chapter, it was discussed how MacIntyre views cooperatives as representing practice conducive institutions. A cooperative necessitates shared decision-making by all the owners of capital, but even this does not ensure a focus on internal goods where the co-operators prioritise external goods such as profit. In the previous chapter, it was noted that MacIntyre refers to shared deliberation and understanding of the goods to be achieved in an institution which supports practices. Cooperatives could support practices, providing their shared deliberations are towards a common good which is the foundation of the organisation and they subordinate external goods to it. Thus, the founding aims of the organisation need to be aligned with the practice and external goods are a consequence of the internal goods of the practice. In small businesses owned by single individuals, there is a lack of shared deliberation as to the good of the organisation as decision-making is based on a single owner of capital. It may be possible for employees in the organisation to pursue a practice, but this would be determined by the owner and what they view as the priority for the business. Practices rely on the purpose of the organisation and its central role in decision-making for their survival by ensuring the hierarchy of goods is maintained whereby external goods are subordinated to internal goods.

Maximisation of Profit or Wealth

One of the most influential economic theories put forward by Milton Friedman (1970) claims that it is the social responsibility of business to maximise profits, within the confines of the law and custom. In as much as Friedman is acknowledging that social responsibility exists in corporations, his view conforms to the standard economic view that economic growth benefits all in the end through maximising value in the firm. Ultimately, when firms engage with socially responsible issues, it is for financial ends since their profits rely on consumer approval which can be influenced by how the firm behaves in relation to society. Companies, large and small are required to focus on wealth creation as the priority; to do otherwise is contrary to the economic view of the purpose of companies. The fundamental issue in this context is that MacIntyre determines the development of virtues through internal goods and as such, businesses which prioritise the external good of wealth, at the expense of internal goods are the antithesis to a practice embodying institution.

Indeed, Beadle (2008) argues that to define business as a practice according to MacIntyre is directly at odds with MacIntyre's views on the system in which businesses operate. Beadle observes that MacIntyre's view of capitalism and its organisations is that there is no distinction between them, that businesses are the institutional representation of capitalism. Beadle argues that capitalists use the surplus value created by workers to further capital interests, rather than benefit workers or the community.

Effectiveness vs. Excellence

MacIntyre (2007), suggests effectiveness is always the priority for running bureaucratic organisations through the allocation of scarce resources to maximise its pre-determined ends. Thus, according to MacIntyre, effectiveness is prioritised in bureaucratic organisations, rather than excellence.

I argue that effectiveness is allowed to dominate because the foundation of such capitalist institutions is based on capital accumulation, rather than some wider benefit to workers or society. Central to MacIntyre is the exercise of the virtues to ensure the practice is sustained and the institution remains in support of the practice. MacIntyre determines that practices are affected by the institution, both positively and negatively and argues that the virtues are essential to ensuring that the institution remains committed to the practice.

For MacIntyre, virtues are necessary for the achievement of internal goods, but that is not to say that external goods are not still genuine goods; in the previous chapter, it was explained how MacIntyre views external goods as goods because they are essential to the existence of a practice. They provide the means to maintaining the institution which sustains the practice. Thus, MacIntyre views external goods as subordinate to internal goods as the latter is the reason for the institution's existence. MacIntyre claims there is a causal relationship between the practice and institution because of the intimacy of the relationship. As a consequence, there is the same intimate relationship between internal and external goods, but because of this, MacIntyre (2007) argues that common goods are at risk, due to the acquisitive nature of the institution. He does point out that the pursuit of internal goods may hinder the achievement of external goods because the manner of society and economy would prevent us from being both virtuous and rich and powerful. Given that the virtues are essential to internal goods and practices, but not to institutions and external goods, if society is dominated by the pursuit of external goods, the cultivation of the virtues will decline (MacIntyre, 2007). Thus, per MacIntyre's approach, the pursuit of internal goods will hinder the pursuit of profits and wealth, which are ultimately the priority in capitalist business and therefore, internal goods will be sacrificed.

MacIntyre uses the example of a child learning to play chess (which was presented in the previous chapter) as the example of internal goods in a practice, which will ideally encourage the child to want to play chess and excel, rather than cheat. It is by no means a given that the child will prefer to stop cheating to obtain candy and excel at chess purely for the sake of the game and the intrinsic benefits it affords. The child may feel that continuing to cheat and obtain the candy is the preferable option. Similarly, in business there must be a commitment to the internal goods to achieve virtue, but the business environment may also encourage such negative behaviour where there is a lack of virtue. According to Maitland (1997), the market encourages conformity to the standard behaviour in the market, in order to survive, which does not include the virtues. This is particularly likely in those organisations which prioritise profit and wealth maximisation. However, he points out that virtues can be evident in the market, but are associated with a private economic benefit, rather than a public good (Maitland, 1997). There are organisations which run contrary to the norms of the capitalist market such as the example used by MacIntyre (2016) of Cummins Engine Company, which did not make a profit for nearly twenty years after its incorporation yet remained in the business of creating diesel engines and once profits were achieved, they were invested in research to improve their product. However, MacIntyre considers that both the owner and investor in the company had an enthusiasm for developing and discovering the potential of diesel engines. As a consequence of such a founding purpose, the organisation remained committed to making an excellent product, suggesting that the purpose of the organisation and its usefulness to society is a factor in maintaining the practice and internal goods as the priority. However, MacIntyre points out that there is pressure in the capitalist market to become ever more profitable which can result in organisations rather different to the Cummins Engine Company example. MacIntyre argues that the virtues are essential to ensuring commitment to the practice. The Anglo-American capitalist system in which businesses operate creates a system of prioritising effectiveness over excellence in which individuals conducting business need to apply differing moral values to get the job done. MacIntyre (1979) refers to a type of 'moral eclecticism' in which workers adopt different moral stances according to the demands of the situation, thus preventing the virtue of consistency. Moore (2012a) gives an account of the history of capitalism in which he concludes that the financial and economic crises of recent history are an inevitable consequence of systemic problems. Furthermore, he gives a damning account of the domination of external goods and the threat to the virtues as a result, at both individual and corporate levels.

In liberal capitalist markets, where there is continual pressure to become more and more profitable, the business would prioritise effectiveness over excellence, thus compromising the very core of the activity which is claimed to be a practice. Beadle (2002) argues that free markets create an inversion of the priorities from institutions and external goods being dependent on the practice and internal goods to the opposite way around. Beadle (2008) argues that MacIntyre views institutions within liberal capitalism as systematically prioritising effectiveness over excellence. According to MacIntyre (2007), a practice requires excellence to be the primary concern to achieve the internal goods associated with said practice. Furthermore, external goods must always be subordinate to the internal goods of the practice to ensure the virtues are maintained. MacIntyre suggests that certain types of organisations can be harmful to the virtues and implicates commercial institutions directly when he refers to Adam Ferguson, a Scottish philosopher of the Enlightenment who also believed that modern commercial society was a threat to the virtues.

Moore (2002) refers to the tension between internal and external goods in business and suggests that MacIntyre's theory helps to explain the working experience for many individuals employed in business. He refers to a type of ethical schizophrenia which limits the capacity of individuals to fully apply their morality to the workplace. Indeed, Jackall (1988) in his study of morality in bureaucratic organisations suggests that the organisational norms, rules and protocols can result in people holding quite different moralities inside the workplace, compared to their privately held views. However, MacIntyre holds that virtues are applied consistently throughout all aspects of an individual's life and there is no balance between internal and external goods, rather there is a strict hierarchy in which external goods are subordinate to internal goods. Moore (2012b) argues that virtuous organisations would sustain a balance between internal and external goods but with an emphasis on internal goods. However, in accordance with MacIntyre, there can be no balancing between goods because external goods must be subordinate to internal goods in the hierarchy. Moore argues that virtues are developed in business and uses the arguments of Hirschman (1982), Maitland (1997) and Warren (1996) to develop this theory. Maitland (1997) claims that virtues such as fairness, sympathy and self-control are rewarded by the market and therefore, those who engage with the market can develop moral characteristics and thus, the market can create and multiply such characteristics. However, this argument is supporting the view that virtues and excellence are a means to a profit-making end, which is contrary to MacIntyre's position. In fact, Maitland argues that it is crucial that virtues should only be fostered where the long-term gains exceed the short-term benefits. Such views have more in common with a management theorist than with the virtue approach of MacIntyre, because it clearly shows how financial objectives are the priority; protecting the company reputation is ultimately for financial ends. Thus, any commitment to internal goods will ultimately be for the promotion of external goods, rather than for a commitment to the virtues or the strict ordering of goods in favour of internal goods. Shaw (1997) disagrees with Maitland's analysis, pointing out that if markets encouraged the virtues, then it would naturally follow that the free market would create virtuous characters and behaviours, which Shaw states is not the case in capitalist society. Warren (1996) argues that communities are the source of understanding the common goods in society, but modern society diminishes capacity for community interaction through a narrowing of commitments which preclude community. He argues that society needs to develop communities and suggests that corporations provide a type of community. Similar to Moore, Warren claims business can be a source of the virtues, claiming that they are key sources of moral development and civic responsibility. Moore, however, is arguing that business itself can be a practice and therefore develop the virtues, whereas Warren is discussing in the context of the workplace as a community and thus refers to the informal exchanges and relationships established within organisations, rather than the formal structure of the organisation. Furthermore, if the workplace is providing an education in virtuous behaviour, there is clear potential for an individual's moral education to be lacking in key areas which do not accord with the company. For example, prudence may not be encouraged in the finance sector, or indeed be discouraged according to MacIntyre who argued that moral character would be detrimental to a financial trader (2015). For MacIntyre, the pursuit of external goods can only lead to the virtues when it is for the promotion of internal goods; external goods pursued for their own sake are not goods and therefore not virtuous.

The mode of work within capitalist business can also impact on the ability to pursue the virtues. MacIntyre (2007) states that most people in modern societies are unable to pursue internal goods in the work that they do. He identifies one of the key moments in modernity and therefore, the erosion of the virtues as when production moved outside the household and employed in the creation of capital. When production is focused on the creation of capital, the virtues are eroded in favour of corporate gain. In a damning indictment of modern business, MacIntyre states that pleonexia is the primary motive of modern productive work. A characteristic of modern production in corporations is the division of labour to achieve the most efficient means of production. Attempts to create greater efficiencies in processes, workflows and productivity date back to the nineteenth century with examples such as Taylorism, developed by Frederick Winslow Taylor transforming the manufacturing industry and the Ford Motor Company's production line. The division of labour requires that a whole task, such as building a machine, is broken down into numerous tasks to achieve more efficient production. Indeed, Adam Smith in the *Wealth of Nations* (1999) refers to the production of pins in a factory, claiming that the division of labour created the most significant improvement in labour production. MacIntyre in his definition of a practice requires that human ability to achieve excellence is developed and that there are standards of excellence which define the activity; none of which could be assigned to a worker packing boxes on a production line. It is not accurate to identify business as a practice, if the majority of people employed in the sustaining of that practice are unable to achieve any internal goods because of the nature of their work. Also, MacIntyre points out the power relationship and the distribution of power as a determining factor in an institution and the impact on practice (Beadle, 2002). It is argued here that capitalist organisations are operated in such a way that capital determines the structure of the organisation to pursue the ends of capital in the form of capital accumulation. Beadle (2008) points out that MacIntyre makes no distinction between capitalism as a system and the companies which operate within the system, describing capitalist enterprises as the means for capitalism. However, MacIntyre (2016) has identified enterprises which, he argues, can achieve the internal and common goods associated with a practice in his examples of Thorupstrand, Cummins Diesel Company and Japanese car manufacturing. Keat (2008) distinguishes between different types of capitalism and suggests that MacIntyre uses liberal capitalism in his examples of the two extremes of fishing crews detailed in the previous chapter. However, the Thorupstrand fishing crew established a cooperative in which they created an alternative ownership and decision-making structure to ensure the goal of the organisation, namely fishing and retaining the community of fishing was the focus. In the next chapter, such alternative forms of organisation will be explored to determine their allegiance to MacIntyre. The Cummins Diesel Company represents an example of a US company which does not conform to the liberal capitalist model because of its commitment to the goal of creating an excellent diesel engine. However, this does not automatically ensure the workers within the organisation are able to pursue a practice because the ownership of the organisation is not devolved to that level whereby workers are able to contribute to the decision-making process. The latter example of the Japanese car manufacturer is based on what Keat (2008) describes as a different form of capitalism, more associated with Germany and Japan. This type of capitalism has different ownership and governance which will positively impact the workforce and the pursuit of practices. However, despite the different ownership and governance giving greater control over practices for the workforce, there must still be a hierarchy of goods in which external goods are subordinated to internal, which is arguably not the case in the Japanese car manufacturing industry. Nevertheless, the focus here is the liberal form of capitalism referred to by MacIntyre, which he clearly is aiming at with his example of the corporate fishing crew.

MacIntyre acknowledges a tension when the institution focuses too much on external goods. However, the overriding purpose for MacIntyre is the internal and common goods to be achieved through the practice and institution relationship. Horvath (1995) points out MacIntyre's use of competition in the Greek sense of striving for excellence, whereas in business, competition is a contest to achieve external goods of material success and individual wealth and power. If in society, where the economic system of capitalism has become dominant, we would value external goods over internal goods, then virtues will no longer have a place in our choices. Sandel (2012) argues that the market has not only encouraged greed but has also expanded into society beyond simple economic exchanges into areas where economics should not venture, such as the sale of human organs. The claim is that society should be protected from the market in certain areas and that not everything should be for sale. The concern about markets relates to the constraints on moral judgement imposed by the market because it is based on efficiency of production and meeting demand. Consequently, whether virtues are encouraged in this type of society is called into question.

Knight (1998) identifies the common feature of MacIntyre's examples of a practice as an internal goal which is common to the practitioners and to achieve them, excellence in one's character is needed to see beyond their immediate needs or desires to a goal that is valued for its own sake. Furthermore, when such goals or goods are achieved, they benefit other practitioners and wider society because they promote the common good in society (Knight, 1998). Clearly, there are examples of business which subvert the prevailing dominance of profit and wealth and instead focus on internal goods as in the example of Thorupstrand fishing community. However, Thorupstrand was established as a cooperative enterprise, operating with a cooperative format where the fishing community are both owners of capital and workers. Decision-making on how to achieve the goals of the enterprise was made through shared deliberation by the community of owner/workers. Unlike corporations with shareholders and their representatives, which are structured to make decisions for the organisation which excludes the views of labour and the generators of capital in favour of the owners of capital. As stated, the purpose of a practice for MacIntyre, is the cultivation of virtues in achieving the internal goods of the practice. In organisations which are structured and operated in a manner which prevents individuals pursuing internal goods, there can be no practice. Such organisations can be operated in such a manner to prevent individuals, in their labour, to achieve internal goods due to a focus on effectiveness determined by the owners of capital. Where an organisation is operated for the benefit of the owners of capital, rather than the producers of capital, there is conflict in the goods to be achieved.

Moore (2002) concludes that MacIntyre is too pessimistic in his view of business organisations and that application of MacIntyre's theory of virtue ethics to business could enable firms to flourish. The basis for his view being that a focus on excellence would enhance corporate performance, rather than reduce it. Moore (2012a) considers MacIntyre's use of tradition in the context of capitalism and refers to the demise of what he termed the alternative to capitalism—communism, which effectively removed any demands on capitalism to moderate or to be found wanting when compared to the alternative. He suggests that using MacIntyre's view of the virtues may present an opportunity to create an alternative model of business in which practices and internal goods are dominant. In the next chapter, the alternatives to capitalism will be analysed to determine their alignment with MacIntyre.

Conclusion

The aim of this chapter was to determine if business can be considered either as a practice or as an institution which sustains practices in accordance with MacIntyre. It has been argued that liberal capitalism encourages an organisational structure in which owners control capital and make decisions based on effectiveness, rather than excellence to achieve greater capital accumulation. Wealth maximisation demands effectiveness over excellence which essentially prevents the development of internal goods through practices and ultimately the virtues. Furthermore, the evidence suggests that far from encouraging the virtues in the workplace, capitalist business encourages an excessive focus on external goods, to the detriment of the virtues. There are exceptions in which the owners of capital strive for excellence in their product or service in preference to capital wealth, as in MacIntyre's example of the Cummins Engine Company. However, MacIntyre argues that shared deliberation and a mutual understanding of common goods are also needed. As identified in the previous chapter, individual goods are understood only in the context of the common good. Indeed, there can be no preconceived idea of an individual good, without first appreciating the common good. MacIntyre uses the example of a cooperative to demonstrate the antithesis to the corporate fishing crew in the previous chapter, which demonstrates MacIntyre values the decision-making structure of the institution and sees it as important to retaining the practice. MacIntyre acknowledges the corrupting power of institutions and it is within liberal capitalism, where the power structure is designed to ensure effectiveness is achieved where this is most clearly demonstrated. The focus on the external goods of capital accumulation prevents the virtues and the internal goods associated with the practice from being achieved. Moore has theorised that business can be a practice and the corporation an institution in accordance with MacIntyre. He argues that virtuous corporations are possible but would require a good purpose which remains the focus for the organisation and external goods are only pursued to ensure the development of the good purpose, articulated through the practice. He points out that business would need to acknowledge responsibility for their influence over society and would require a conducive environment in relation to regulations, market, labour and capital. Moore acknowledges that currently, businesses within capitalism would need a radical change to conform with his virtuous organisation theory. However, it has been argued here that business cannot be a practice in accordance with MacIntyre. Furthermore, Moore argues that businesses which can demonstrate the correct balance between internal and external goods can be virtuous, but MacIntyre identifies a rank ordering of goods in his teleological approach in which external goods are always subordinate to internal goods.

The environment for practice bearing institutions will be explored in later chapters. As suggested in the introduction to this chapter, there are alternative forms of capitalism and alternative forms of institution which may embody practices to a greater or lesser extent; such alternatives will be explored in the next chapter.

References

Beadle, R. (2002). The misappropriation of MacIntyre. *Reason in Practice, 2*, 45–54.

Beadle, R. (2008). Why business cannot be a practice. *Analyse & Kritik, 1*, 1–13.

Friedman, M. (1970, September 13). The social responsibility of business is to increase its profits. *The New York Times Magazine.*

Hall, P., & Soskice, F. (2001). An introduction to varieties of capitalism. In P. Hall & F. Soskice (Eds.), *Varieties of capitalism: The institutional foundations of comparative advantage* (pp. 1–70). Oxford University Press.

Hirschman, A. (1982). Rival interpretations of market society: Civilising, destructive, or feeble? *Journal of Economic Literature, 20*(4), 1463–1484.

Horvath, C. M. (1995). Excellence V. effectiveness: MacIntyre's critique of business. *Business Ethics Quarterly, 3*(1), 499–532.

Jackall, R. (1988). *Moral mazes: The world of corporate managers*. Oxford University Press.

Keat, R. (2008). Practices, firms and varieties of capitalism. *Philosophy of Management, 7*(1), 77–91.

Knight, K. (1998). *The MacIntyre reader*. Polity Press.

MacIntyre, A. (1979). Corporate modernity and moral judgement: Are they mutually exclusive? In K. E. Goodpaster & K. M. Sayre (Eds.), *Ethics and problems of the 21st century* (pp. 122–135). University of Notre Dame Press.

MacIntyre, A. (2007). *After virtue* (3rd ed.). University of Notre Dame Press.

MacIntyre, A. (2016). *Ethics in the conflicts of modernity: An essay on desire, practical reasoning and narrative*. Cambridge University Press.

Maitland, I. (1997). Virtuous markets: The market as school of the virtues. *Business Ethics Quarterly, 7*(1), 7–31.

Moore, G. (2002). On the implications of the practice-institution distinction: MacIntyre and the application of modern virtue ethics to business. *Business Ethics Quarterly, 12*(1), 19–32.

Moore, G. (2005a). Humanizing business: A modern virtue ethics approach. *Business Ethics Quarterly, 15*(2), 237–255.

Moore, G. (2005b). Corporate character: Modern virtue ethics and the virtuous corporation. *Business Ethics Quarterly, 15*(4), 659–685.

Moore, G. (2008). Re-imagining the morality of management: A modern virtue ethics approach. *Business Ethics Quarterly, 18*(4), 483–511.

Moore, G. (2012a). The virtue of governance, the governance of virtue. *Business Ethics Quarterly, 22*(2), 293–318.

Moore, G. (2012b). Virtue in business: Alliance boots and an empirical exploration of MacIntyre's conceptual framework. *Organization Studies, 33*(3), 363–387.

Moore, G. (2015). Corporate character, corporate virtues. *Business Ethics: A European Review, 24*(2), 99–114.

Sandel, M. (2012). *What money can't buy: The moral limits of markets*. Penguin Books Ltd.

Shaw, B. (1997). Sources of virtue: The market and the community. *Business Ethics Quarterly, 7*(1), 33–50.

Smith, A. (1999). *The wealth of nations books I–III*. Penguin Books Ltd.

Warren, R. C. (1996). The empty company: Morality and job security. *Personnel Review, 25*, 41–53.

CHAPTER 4

Alternative Forms of Enterprise Within and Without Capitalism and MacIntyre

Introduction

If the monetary priorities of capitalist business are considered antithetical to practices as argued in the previous chapters, it is then necessary to explore alternative business environments where practices could be encouraged within institutions. There are institutions operating within market systems which do not conform to a capitalist requirement for profit in the same way, which can be assessed for their application of a MacIntyrean approach to virtue. The purpose of this chapter is to identify the extent to which these different types of organisations are consistent with MacIntyre. To this end, Moore's virtuous business characterisation will be employed, as will the alternatives such as coordinated market economies of Germany and Japan be considered (Keat, 2008) together with cooperatives and community projects identified by MacIntyre (2016) as sources of practice and common goods.

MacIntyre considers that institutions are responsible for the corruption or lack of emphasis on practice, where the external goods of wealth and power are prioritised over the practice. Hence, Moore and Beadle (2006) suggest that key to applying MacIntyre is a focus on the institution. The previous chapter has highlighted the forces of capitalism as being such that financial rewards take precedence over the practice, which is counter to MacIntyre in which the internal goods of the practice are dominant over external goods in a strict hierarchical ordering. External

G. Hall, *Virtue and Social Enterprise*,
https://doi.org/10.1007/978-3-031-14027-3_4

goods should only be pursued to the extent that they will sustain the practices. However, there are institutions which operate alongside capitalism which may not subscribe to the same demands to gain external goods, to the detriment of the practice. Such institutions and how they are organised and structured, and how they resist corruption from internal pressure to wealth maximise and the external forces of the market and competition, will be considered in this chapter within the context of MacIntyre. Moore (2005b) devised a set of characteristics which embody the cardinal virtues espoused by MacIntyre, which, if in place, would create an institution which is in good order. However, unlike Moore, it is the intention here to relate MacIntyre not to capitalist businesses but to those alternative organisations which are potentially, more likely to meet his criteria. MacIntyre (2016) cites examples of such organisations in his work which have been discussed, such as the fishing crews of Thorupstrand and the community organising of Monte Azul. Inherent to the exploration of practice nurturing institutions is their focus on common goods because of the relationship between the internal goods being reliant on an understanding of the common goods at stake in a practice; common goods are prior to internal goods, as previously discussed. Identified previously are the elements MacIntyre determines are necessary for the politics of making and sustaining of communities, these too will be discussed in this context. It is contended here that alternative forms of economic activity such as cooperatives can embody MacIntyre's practice-institution, providing they consider the wider issues of common good, power balance and the political economy in which they operate.

The Virtuous Corporation

Moore (2005b) acknowledges MacIntyre's concern about capitalist organisations focusing on external goods, to the detriment of internal goods, but suggests that a virtuous corporate character would enable the balance between external and internal goods to be maintained to protect the practice. He argues that MacIntyre's work as detailed in Chapter 2 is useful in highlighting the corruption which is possible in corporations where external goods are the priority. However, it has been argued in the previous chapter that capitalist corporations are not conducive with MacIntyre. Furthermore, creating a balance between external and internal goods as Moore suggest is contrary to MacIntyre's view that there should be a hierarchy of goods, with external goods being subordinate to internal goods; there is no allowance for any sense of balance. Wicks (1997) argues that a radical change would be required in our economic and cultural practices to be able to apply MacIntyre's theory to business. Wicks' view, according to Dobson (1997), relies on the belief that MacIntyre blames the state of modern society on individualism, acquisitiveness and market values. Wicks does not agree that modernity as defined by MacIntyre is as dire as he describes. He suggests that modern companies and the individuals who work within them are not so clearly categorised in terms of their virtue or vice. He suggests there are many examples of people who would prioritise internal goods over material gains and that MacIntyre uses extreme examples, particularly in the fishing crew analogy (Wicks, 1997). However, Dobson argues against Wicks' view of MacIntyre and suggests that in the fishing crew analogy it was a deliberate example of extremes, which does not necessarily deny the presence of a range of examples in between the extremes. He suggests that MacIntyre's use of the fishing example implies that virtue ethics could be applied to a business activity, with positive results. Clearly, there is disagreement about applying MacIntyre to capitalist business, from dismissal of the appropriateness of its use in such a context, to the extent to which it can be applied to such businesses.

In accordance with MacIntyre and my arguments in the previous chapter, it is my view that capitalist business must prioritise external goods as a means to the end of profit and wealth within the capitalist free market and therefore, businesses cannot be practices. Moore argues that his virtuous corporation theory is not exclusively for capitalist corporations, but also more generally, for organisations to embrace the concept of virtue and it is for this purpose that his theory is explored in this chapter. MacIntyre (1994) views the mode of institutionalisation as influencing the extent to which practices can be prioritised because they can allow external goods such as money and power to influence the practice. Thus, Moore (2005) suggests, a better understanding of the institution and its structure and processes will better enable the assessment of what features are needed to nurture the practice. Furthermore, he argues that individual virtues, as MacIntyre discusses, can be supplemented with institutional level virtues which can give a conceptualisation of institutional character. He argues that a virtuous corporate character can protect practices from the corrupting influence of institutions and the excessive pursuit of external goods.

Moore's study on corporate character explores the relationship and tension between internal and external goods and practice-institution in a corporate context, and the consequent negative effects on individual and common goods. His aim is to establish the corporate characteristics which, if they exist in a company, would create an organisation which was able to balance practice and excellence with institution and effectiveness. The focus for Moore (2005b) is the institution and its structure and purpose, rather than the individual, because of its potential to thwart individual pursuit of excellence in practice by prioritising the external goods of power and wealth. The basic requirements of a virtuous corporation rely on a reiteration of MacIntyre; core function is to sustain the practice, excellence, external goods only in support of practice, and good character. He further adds that a just purpose with a power-balanced structure, with transparency of governance and a culture which is supportive of the virtues. The virtues of fortitude, temperance, justice, prudence, integrity and constancy are also essential for a virtuous corporation according to Moore (2005). Moore supports the prioritisation of practice and encouragement of excellence, with only enough emphasis on external goods to an extent which is sufficient to sustain the institution and therefore, the practice and, to have the character to resist the corrupting power of related organisations.

Beadle (2002) argues that a fuller understanding of MacIntyre is needed, beyond the practice, to include the essential elements of the common good, the importance of power in the institutional structure and to appreciate MacIntyre's view of the political economy. MacIntyre supports the smaller scale institutions which he claims encourage the virtues and cites examples of fishing communities and Welsh mining communities where commitment to practices is a communal issue whereby decisions about priorities are shared. The question in this chapter is whether there are such organisations which conform with MacIntyre, which can also claim allegiance to his wider views relating to the common good, power balance and the political economy. Moore's conceptual framework for a virtuous organisation is helpful in identifying characteristics which could relate to MacIntyre, providing that the goods of the practice are always the priority for the organisation and there is no trade-off between internal and external goods. However, Moore oscillates between references to balancing goods and prioritising goods which is contrary to MacIntyre's position that there is a strict rank ordering in which external goods are always subordinate to internal goods. It is my argument that capitalist organisations, even when they have a regard for internal goods are creating a balance of goods which is contrary to MacIntyre's position. Beadle (2002) is unequivocal on MacIntyre's views and suggests that capitalism in such a form cannot support the virtues because of the dominance of effectiveness and the pursuit of power.

Virtues in Business Type Institutions

Dawson and Bartholomew (2003) consider the question of profit and its role within markets and argue that it is trade, through the exchange of goods, rather than profit which is necessary for the distribution of goods through a community to ensure that needs are met. The exchange of goods between people with different skills has been happening throughout history and money used as a form of exchange without profit being an essential element. Indeed, they argue that trade is essential to a practice because of the requirement to exchange goods between communities and individuals. Thus, Dawson and Bartholomew conclude that there is still a role for business in the development of a practice because profit is not an essential part of trade and exchange and precede the development of capitalist economies. However, it has already been noted that capitalism does not encourage such a position. As such, it is worthwhile to explore the tenability of institutions operating within a market system which do not subscribe to acquisitiveness of capitalist markets. If Moore's characterisation of a virtuous corporation is imposed on an institution which is not subject to the capitalist market focus on external goods, is the institution less flawed and useful as an insight into the type of institution which could embody a practice? MacIntyre's fishing crew discussed in Chapter 2 suggest that despite operating a form of business which is engaged in achieving a profit, such organisations can be practice embodying where the primary objective remains the practice. However, this raises the question of what type of institution is supporting such a fishing crew in their pursuit of the practice, which leads back to MacIntyre as a guide. MacIntyre makes clear that institutions are necessary for the support and flourishing of a practice. However, for the practice to flourish it is essential that it is viewed as the priority by the institution.

The mode of institutionalisation has already been identified as critical earlier in the chapter, whereby decision-making, both in terms of power structure and the organisational purpose are key influences on the practice. Moore and Beadle (2006) suggest that the environment in terms of the market, regulations, labour and capital, influences the focus on the practice. They do, however, highlight that institutions are able to withstand their environment in certain circumstances and they elaborate on a case study of Traidcraft plc to assess their virtuous organisation framework (Moore & Beadle, 2006). Essentially, they use the example of a Fairtrade organisation to test out their tripartite classification; Traidcraft plc is a trading business with ethical concerns relating to poverty in the developing world, which was originally formed from a charitable organisation and still retains its roots through a charity and a charitable foundation alongside the trading company. Moore and Beadle argue that Traidcraft plc has a just purpose and through its principles and mission it retains a focus on internal goods, profits being viewed as a means to an end, rather than an end in itself. However, they indicate that the organisation does not always prioritise internal goods by stating that losses in previous years have created a greater focus on profits (Moore & Beadle, 2006).

Dawson and Bartholomew (2003) argue that practices in the MacIntyrean sense requires trading in various forms because people have to specialise in their practices and therefore will need to exchange goods and services to meet their living needs and the needs of the community. They argue that profits create the problem in relating business to MacIntyre, unlike trade, which can take the form of barter or monetary payment without the need for profit. Furthermore, they argue that business can be virtuous if it subordinates the pursuit of profit to a community-based good. They question whether it is naïve to suggest that society could adopt a business approach which subordinates profit to the common good of community, but also point out that central to MacIntyre's view of virtue is the need to encourage society in which virtues flourish. They argue that developing a conceptual framework for virtuous business creates an alternative to what business currently looks like in the dominance of capitalism, which is necessary before any reform could take place.

Common Goods

Dupre (1993) makes clear the Aristotelian view of common goods as those shared by a community and can only be achieved through community, rather than through individuals pursuing their own interests. Solomon (1997) indicates that Aristotelian virtue tells us that it is not through individual self-interest that virtues are achieved, it is through cooperation towards the wellbeing of a community that individual excellence can be achieved. MacIntyre reinforces this view and makes explicit the importance of common goods being prior to individual goods. Indeed, individual goods cannot be conceived without the understanding and cooperation required for the achievement of common goods, which Aristotle defined as eudaimonia or human flourishing (Sison & Fontrodona, 2012). MacIntyre is very specific that his meaning for common goods is not simply a sum of individual parts, but those derived from shared experience and cooperative actions.

Coe and Beadle (2008) outline an approach using MacIntyre as the basis for empirical study of The Sage Gateshead and extend the relationship beyond the practice and institution, to community-based projects. They view The Sage Gateshead as a practice-embodying institution because of its focus on common goods within a community setting. They regard the institution as representing a positive reflection of MacIntyre's view of the virtues and suggest that it could develop the common good and flourishing through the practice of making music in a community context. It is important to note that the organisation is not a corporate entity but owned by Gateshead Council and run by a Trust; it has a mission to widen access to the participation, learning and enjoyment of a broad range of music.

Finchett-Maddock (2008) argues that the social centre movement in the UK are examples of MacIntyrean, practice-based small communities. The Social Centre Network (UK) describe such places as where capitalism can be challenged through collective action. Finchett-Maddock invokes MacIntyre's views on a politics of local community to argue that they play a political role in the development of a community. MacIntyre suggests that such an institution would be outside of the market economy in which so much economic activity is conducted in modern society. The social centres provide for a range of activities, both cultural and political, for those within the community and they also reach out to those outside it. Their ethos is to create a community which develops virtues in political and communal discourse and action to further the alternatives to capitalism. Finchett-Maddock argues that such groups are representative of MacIntyre's view of Utopia whereby they live outside of consumer society and advance the ideals of community and attempt to insulate themselves from the influence of capitalism. Blackledge (2009) writing about MacIntyre and Marxism suggests that it is capitalism at the root of peoples' inability to be virtuous due to the exploitative nature of capitalism as a means to creating wealth at the expense of labour. Furthermore, he argues, there is a misunderstanding, perpetuated by the capitalist system, that leads people to believe that success is measured through the acquisition of external goods. Blackledge describes this as a reversal in the understanding of virtues and vices in which the pursuit of external goods is seen as a virtue. He also points out that MacIntyre views capitalism and the free market as thwarting the ability of individuals to develop communities in which the common goods can be deliberated and pursued. O'Brien (2009) supports the view that capitalism discourages an appreciation of the common good in his research in the context of business and argues that Western society encourages individualism and shared goods are resisted.

Subsequently, the organisations researched which demonstrate a closer alignment with MacIntyre tend to be those not fitting the criteria for a capitalist corporation. These organisations have an overt commitment to community benefits as distinct from profit motives. Supporting this, Beadle (2008) suggests that the modern capitalist market is imposed on labour and production, rather than driven by the common good. The implication is that organisations with a clear mission to further community or social benefits may embody MacIntyre's virtues.

Alternative Forms of Institution and Economy

Keat argues that institutions embodied in different types of capitalism vary in the extent to which they are impacted by acquisitiveness and competition and identifies that MacIntyre does not take issue with external goods because he believes in their institutional role in developing practices. Therefore, the problem with capitalism, for MacIntyre, must be related to the nature of capitalist institutions and their influence on the practice and goods. In his use of Hall and Soskice's (2001) work, he cites the key differences between the two types as being based on share ownership, governance and cooperation rather than competition. In the LME of the UK, according to Keat, the dominant shareholders are pension funds and similar which hold a relatively small number of shares in a number of different companies, with managers who are incentivised to use a short-term approach to the profits of the companies they invest in. Whereas in Germany, the CME has companies and banks as the major shareholders which tend to hold a large number of shares in less companies and have a longer-term view of corporate strategies, alongside the financial results (Keat, 2008). There tends to be more hierarchy in LMEs compared to a more consensual form of management which consider both shareholders and workforce in CMEs (Keat, 2008). CMEs tend to demonstrate greater cooperation between firms than LMEs which tend towards competition (Keat, 2008). The focus in this research is the liberal market economy of the UK and USA and the associated issues with share ownership and governance and cooperation.

Stiglitz (2009) argues that a more balanced range of institutional types are needed in a society, rather than simply free markets and government. He argues from an historical perspective that past successes and failures in societies with different modes of institution can demonstrate the best balance. He claims that neoliberalism in which individual self-interest dominated has not been successful; however, countries which demonstrate a range of institutional types, including small-scale enterprises based in towns or villages and cooperatives, have been. He claims that the social cooperative economy is successful in creating an environment which nurtures democracy and intrinsic rewards. This view can be assimilated with MacIntyre's view of practice and the institutional form which best supports it. Further, his position is heavily influenced by the role of community and its historical context (MacIntyre, 2016). Clearly, the historical context is key to understanding, particularly in relation to the cooperative movement which preceded the modern cooperative enterprise. It is, therefore, necessary to explore alternative organisational forms such as cooperatives, MacIntyre cites examples of cooperatives as practice supporting institutions, thus an exploration of this type of institution is warranted.

Cooperatives as Practice Embodying Institutions

As mentioned in the previous chapters, MacIntyre recounts the story of Thorupstrand in which a fishing community with a significant history in shared fishing created a cooperative when faced with legislation to privatise fishing quotas to individual boats. The cooperative company made up of twenty families purchased a common pool of quotas, with decisions being democratically based on one member–one vote with responsibility for maintaining the practice of share fishing being jointly assumed by all the families. The practice of share fishing was already a cooperative activity through maintaining the boats and the supporting structure of the community which relied on fishing and with all earnings and losses being shared proportionately amongst the crew. However, the purchase of a common pool of quotas gave rise to a more formal structure to the cooperation. MacIntyre (2016) considers the virtues that were essential to its success as the qualities of mind and character by those involved in the new cooperative; prudence, justice, courage and temperateness as essential virtues, without which the venture would likely have failed. He also remarks on the close association between family and the workplace and suggests that there is understanding of the common good and how they are related across the different aspects of the community life. Efficiency and growth in such a cooperative are understood differently to capitalist organisations because they are not based solely on the financial rewards, but rather, on a regard for the flourishing of the community as a whole.

Cooperative enterprises have a long history dating back to the fifteenth century when democratic ownership and equal distribution of wealth manifested in The Diggers movement which took over waste land for cultivation for common interests (Spreckley, 1981). The Rochdale Society of Equitable Pioneers in 1844 was founded on democratic principles with ownership resting with the members of the cooperative to provide goods which were unadulterated and not overpriced (Rochdale Pioneers Museum 2018). The focus for the Rochdale Pioneers extended beyond the provision of goods to the consumer, to the interests of the wider community (Spreckley, 1981); the Rochdale Pioneers were also known for encouraging the expansion and creation of other cooperatives (Reeve et al., 2004). A more recent example of cooperatives is MONDRAGON which was founded in 1956 and has since grown into one of the world's largest industrial cooperative associations. It is founded on cooperative principles and success is attributed to the priority of labour over capital (Heales et al., 2017). The Co-operative principles are briefly described as:

- Voluntary organisations with membership open to all persons
- Democratic organisations based on participation and control by members
- Democratic control of capital and surplus allocated for co-operative purposes, rather than to owners
- Autonomous organisations controlled by members
- Providing education to members and the general public to promote understanding and benefits of co-operation
- Work with other co-operatives to strengthen the movement

- Member's decisions based on promoting sustainable communities.

(Paraphrased from Reeve et al., 2004)

There is broad alignment between the cooperative principles identified above and MacIntyre's view of the necessary elements for creating communities, which were discussed in Chapter 2 in relation to common goods and the politics of making and sustaining of local communities. Co-operatives share an important feature with MacIntyre regarding democratic decision-making in the interests of the community. The community in the cooperative sense incorporates the organisation, community, the cooperative movement and other cooperatives. MacIntyre views shared deliberation in the interests of the community as essential to the making and sustaining of communities, as is a shared conception of what goods are at stake and how they can be achieved. The cooperative movement shares a purpose in promoting sustainable communities according to Reeve et al. (2004). Shared deliberation and relevant voices are heard through open membership and democratic decision-making and participation, which also facilitates agreement on the goods at stake and how they would best be achieved. Democratic control of capital to ensure there is no undue power or influence.

Spreckley (1981) argues that the traditional definition of a workers' cooperative as controlled and owned by labour is too narrow to fully explain their community role and their internal functioning. A greater understanding of their community and political influence is needed to capture the importance of MacIntyre's ideas for the creation of communities. Furthermore, cooperatives are not the only form of organisation which may align with MacIntyre's practice and community. In the next chapter, social enterprise will be discussed in depth to determine its significance to MacIntyre's approach to virtues through practices and common goods and will be positioned in relation to its role within the economic and social environment and its historical context.

Conclusion

Moore argues that virtuous corporations are those which prioritise excellence in practice, without allowing the acquisitiveness of the institution to become dominant. However, Moore does not use the hierarchical approach of MacIntyre in which external goods must always be subordinate to internal goods and common goods. This ordering of goods is fundamental to MacIntyre's position for the pursuit of virtues. Moore and Beadle consider Traidcraft plc as an organisation in a case study in which they conclude that it could be deemed a virtuous corporation because it meets the characteristics defined by Moore. However, there remains the wider context of MacIntyre's work in which the community and political role of a practice embodying institution are considered by the organisation. To this end, alternative forms of institutions, including cooperatives, are considered and the extent to which they exhibit commitment to these key elements of MacIntyre's work. The cooperative model can be applied to a range of organisations from industrial to the arts, as demonstrated by MONDRAGON with its diverse projects. MacIntyre positions the virtues associated with practices within a wider view which includes community, the common good and the role of politics in determining the extent a community can flourish. Thus, organisations which are embedded in communities are considered a source of possible practice embodying institutions, such as social enterprises. MacIntyre cites examples of cooperatives as embodying the balance between practice, virtue and the institution and critically, these types of organisations have an historical context based in communal support, democratic involvement and arguably a political role in the making and sustaining of communities. A broader term which encompasses cooperatives and other forms of trading organisation with a social purpose is social enterprise. These organisations contribute to the common good through their purpose and foster democratic power structures to ensure that organisational goals achieve the common good. Social enterprises will be considered in greater detail in the next chapter as it is contended that such organisations could represent practice embodying institutions in the MacIntyrean sense.

References

Beadle, R. (2002). The misappropriation of MacIntyre. *Reason in Practice, 2*, 45–54.

Beadle, R. (2008). Why business cannot be a practice. *Analyse & Kritik, 1*, 1–13.

Blackledge, P. (2009). Alasdair MacIntyre: Social practices, Marxism and ethical anti-capitalism. *Political Studies, 57*, 866–884.

Coe, S., & Beadle, R. (2008). Could we know a practice-embodying institution if we saw one? *Philosophy of Management, 7*(1), 9–19.

Dawson, D., & Bartholomew, C. (2003). Virtues, managers and business people: Finding a place for MacIntyre in a business context. *Journal of Business Ethics, 48*, 127–138.

Dobson, J. (1997). MacIntyre's position on business: A response to Wicks. *Business Ethics Quarterly, 7*(4), 125–132.

Dupre, L. (1993). The common good and the open society. *The Review of Politics, 55*(4), 687–712.

Finchett-Maddock, L. (2008). An anarchist's Wetherspoons or virtuous resistance? Social centres as MacIntyre's vision of practice-based communities. *Philosophy of Management, 7*, 21–31.

Hall, P., & Soskice, F. (2001). An introduction to varieties of capitalism. In P. Hall & F. Soskice (Eds.), *Varieties of capitalism: The institutional foundations of comparative advantage* (pp. 1–70). Oxford University Press.

Heales, C., Hodgson, M., & Rich, H. (2017). *Humanity at work: MONDRAGON, a social innovation ecosystem case study*. The Young Foundation.

Keat, R. (2008). Practices, firms and varieties of capitalism. *Philosophy of Management, 7*(1), 77–91.

MacIntyre, A. (1994). A partial response to my critics. In J. Horton & S. Mendus (Eds.), *After MacIntyre* (pp. 283–304). Polity Press.

MacIntyre, A. (2016). *Ethics in the conflicts of modernity: An essay on desire, practical reasoning and narrative*. Cambridge University Press.

Moore, G. (2005a). Humanizing business: A modern virtue ethics approach. *Business Ethics Quarterly, 15*(2), 237–255.

Moore, G. (2005b). Corporate character: Modern virtue ethics and the virtuous corporation. *Business Ethics Quarterly, 15*(4), 659–685.

Moore, G., & Beadle, R. (2006). In search of organisational virtue in business: Agents, goods, practices, institutions and environments. *Organisational Studies, 27*(3), 369–389.

O'Brien, T. (2009). Reconsidering the common good in a business context. *Journal of Business Ethics, 85*(1), 25–37.

Reeve, D., Brooke, C., & Williams, S. (2004). *Management case study biography of the co-operative bank*. University of Lincoln.

Sison, J. G., & Fontrodona, J. (2012). The common good of the firm in the Aristotelian-Thomistic tradition. *Business Ethics Quarterly, 22*(2), 211–246.

Solomon R. C. (1997). Corporate roles, personal virtues: An Aristotelian approach to business ethics. In D. Statman (Ed.), *Virtue ethics: A critical reader*. Edinburgh University Press.

Spreckley, F. (1981). *Social audit: A management tool for co-operative working*. Beechwood College.

Stiglitz, D. J. (2009). Moving beyond market fundamentalism to a more balanced economy. *Annals of Public and Cooperative Economics, 80*(3), 345–360.

Wicks, A. C. (1997). On MacIntyre, modernity and the virtues: A response to Dobson. *Business Ethics Quarterly, 7*(4), 133–135.

CHAPTER 5

Defining Social Enterprise

Introduction

The previous chapter considered alternative forms of enterprise which may be more compatible with MacIntyre. In this chapter, social enterprise and its role within the economy will be discussed to explore its ability to be a practice conducive institution, compatible with MacIntyre. Social enterprise in the UK and Europe can be viewed as part of the social economy and this too will be explored to determine its pertinence to MacIntyre's work. MacIntyre cites examples of cooperatives as practice-based institutions; social enterprise may present a wider body of organisations which can embody his views. Significantly, social enterprises also have an historical context based on communal support, democratic involvement and a political role both at national and local levels. This chapter explores the existing literature regarding social enterprise and its emergence in recent years. The aim is to establish the current context for social enterprise and to explore the characteristics which are representative of this type of organisation. This is particularly important given the variety of definitions available for social enterprises (Grant & Dart, 2009). Furthermore, the environment and historical context in which social enterprises are positioned will be discussed to establish their role within the wider economy. Social enterprise is a modern term for a business organisation which is distinguished by its social aims (Social Enterprise Coalition, 2003). This chapter will consider the key characteristics of

G. Hall, *Virtue and Social Enterprise*,
https://doi.org/10.1007/978-3-031-14027-3_5

a social enterprise developed most comprehensively by the European Research Network (EMES); the spectrum approach developed by Dees (1996, 1998) and further elaborated by Alter (2010) and Pearce's (2003) theory of 'radical' and 'reformist' approaches of social enterprises.

There is a great deal of discussion surrounding the definition of what constitutes a social enterprise but there is a general recognition that it is a hybrid organisation which has a business model requiring the generation of profit, in order to fulfil its social aims (EMES, 2001; Pearce, 2003). The classification and emphasis of social enterprise vary in different countries, for example, in the UK it is described as an organisation which is profit-making, but its primary concern is to create social benefits, rather than prioritising profit maximisation for its owners. The UK incorporated a new legal form called the Community Interest Company (CIC) in 2004. This is a limited liability company which has been designed specifically for social enterprises (CIC Regulator, 2008). The CIC does not replace existing types of social enterprise such as cooperatives and credit unions but provides an additional legal form for social enterprises which want to adopt a limited company status. In the USA, there is also an emphasis on the business objectives of the social enterprise. According to research, social enterprises in the USA have a greater emphasis on their commercial activities compared to other countries (Henry et al., 2006). In contrast, Italy created a legal form of social cooperative in 2005 which places the emphasis on the cooperative nature of the enterprise (Defourny & Nyssens, 2008); the essential characteristic of the cooperative being the sharing of responsibilities and benefits between members, rather than profit-making being a means to the end of meeting social aims. Indeed, (as noted in Chapter 1) it was in Italy that the concept of a social enterprise was first established in 1990s, following the cooperative initiatives which had developed in the late 1980s (Defourny & Nyssens, 2008). These cooperatives differed from traditional forms in that they were made up of different categories of stakeholders, such as volunteers and paid employees, rather than collective ownership as in a cooperative in which all members are owners. The legal form of 'social co-operative' was created to address issues in work access for disadvantaged people and delivery of social, health and educational services. The legal form was further developed with a law in 2005 which broadened the scope to incorporate 'social utility' (Defourny & Nyssens, 2008). This extended the legal status of social enterprise to organisations which satisfied the criteria of stakeholder representation and restricted profit distribution.

The emphasis on the cooperative status of social enterprises is reiterated in other European countries; Spain, Portugal, Greece, France and Belgium all have created legal forms which are based on a cooperative structure (Defourny & Nyssens, 2008). This distinction can have important implications in terms of definition; UK and the USA focus on business character, whereas the Italian model emphasises the stakeholder role in governance. However, to focus only on the legal frameworks for social enterprise would ignore a significant number of organisations which operate as a social enterprise through their social function, rather than their legal status. It is this variety of form which characterises social enterprise as a sector (ECOTEC, 2003).

Following from the above the purpose of this chapter is to explore the differing definitions of social enterprise in relation to their role as a practice embodying institution; the focus of the organisation is clearly central to the ability to nurture a practice. Social enterprise as an umbrella term encompasses a number of different organisations which may be practice encouraging in MacIntyrean terms, to different extents or not at all. To this end, the organisational roles and contexts will be explored. Furthermore, there are differing views on whether social enterprise can be viewed on a spectrum of organisations which includes capitalist corporations within it (Young & Lecy, 2012). Or indeed, social enterprises should not be considered in the same context as capitalist businesses at all and should be viewed as an alternative form of business (Pearce, 2003). These arguments will be explored to determine the compatibility of social enterprises with MacIntyre's work.

Problems with Definition in Social Enterprise Research

One of the issues encountered with research into social enterprise has been the difficulty in characterising what constitutes a social enterprise (Martin & Thompson, 2010). The sheer variety and form of these organisations create difficulties in identifying a model for the basis of research. There are many examples of organisations which can be defined as a social enterprise through their mission and profit structure. Social objectives can include community-based initiatives which aim to improve living standards or employment prospects in either local communities or developing economies. Equally, environmental issues can be considered social objectives in relation to recycling, preservation and organic farming, to name a few issues amongst others.

The EMES International Research Network (EMES) has published several books and working papers on social enterprise in Europe (Borzaga & Defourny, 2001; Defourny & Nyssens, 2008; Nyssens, 2006). The EMES network is made up of university research centres and individual researchers with a shared focus on third sector research. The EMES Network considers social enterprises to be part of the third sector due to the social objectives associated with their formation and profit distribution criteria (EMES, 2001). The third sector has also been identified with the concept of a social economy in which individuals form an association or society in order to address social disadvantage. The European Commission's Social Economy Unit includes social enterprises, cooperatives, mutual societies, associations and foundations in the definition of the social economy (Doherty et al., 2009). The key elements to organisations within the social economy are defined by Defourny and Beveltere (1999) as being governed by four principles; community before profit, autonomy of management, decision-making is democratic and people are prioritised over capital.

The importance of these principles is critical to understanding the difference between the organisations which make up the social economy, government bodies and mainstream business. Social Enterprise organisations in this sector are established in response to a social need and profits are required in order to continue and contribute to the social end, it is not primarily required to pay returns to investors. There is no direct government involvement to dictate actions and therefore management is autonomous. Democratic decision-making is an important element because it is based on the individual's right to vote, rather than the amount of capital owned determining one's entitlement to vote in decisions. The last principle requires that people and the social objectives of the organisation are given priority when surpluses are distributed, rather than profits for shareholders.

In response to all the above, we might argue then that social enterprise is encompassed in the social economy and includes a variety of organisational types. The types of social enterprise can be broadly categorised in the following types of organisations:

- Social firm—whose specific purpose is to employ people who are disadvantaged in the labour market.
- Development trust—community-based enterprises which are involved in community regeneration.
- Community Development Financial Institution (CDFI)—a financial services provider to business and social economy organisations, which has social objectives.
- Cooperative—an association or business which is owned and controlled by a group of people for their mutual benefit.
- Credit Unions—financial services in the third sector providing savings and loan facilities to members using the cooperative system.
- Community or social businesses—established to provide opportunities for employment or services to a community.
- Micro-finance—the provision of small loans and savings facilities to individuals and business ventures for those on low incomes.
- Housing associations—organisations which provide affordable housing for those on low income, with surpluses reinvested into housing construction and maintenance.
- Employee owned businesses—companies which are owned by the employees, either fully, or with a substantial interest.
- Intermediate labour markets.
- Charities and voluntary organisations with income primarily from trading activities.

(Paraphrased from Martin & Thompson, 2010, Pearce, 2003)

Research Approaches in the Field of Social Enterprise

There is debate regarding the conceptual understanding of social enterprise, ranging from comparisons of their form incorporating socioeconomic context (Kerlin, 2006) to a typology of social enterprise (Alter, 2010). Emerging from such research are several schools of thought which attempt to harness and explain the concept of social enterprise. They include classification of key characteristics within an 'ideal-type' framework (Spear & Bidet, 2003); a spectrum of organisational types which range from profit maximising, socially responsible businesses, social enterprises and charities (Alter, 2010); a social innovation emphasis in which social goals are achieved through entrepreneurial activities, with no defining organisational form (Young, 1983); social enterprise as a hybrid organisation whereby they combine features of public sector, private sector and non-profit organisations (Doherty et al., 2014); and a 'zoo' analogy focusing on diversity in which commercial and social interests intersect in many different guises such as socially responsible corporations, commercial non-profit organisations and social cooperatives (Young & Lecy, 2012). The key characteristic or 'ideal' type' and spectrum schools of thought are the most widely cited approaches and will be explored further to create a conceptual understanding of social enterprise. This understanding is necessary because one of the key arguments being advanced in this research is that social enterprises have a fundamentally different values framework from first sector, private companies. This is borne of a number of historical and contextual factors which will be explored in this and later chapters. There is divergence in the theory of social enterprise in terms of how and why social enterprise came into existence and focusing on the key characteristics and spectrum approaches clearly highlights this difference.

Social Enterprise Schools of Thought

Social Enterprise Defined Through Key Indicators or Characteristics

The European Thematic Network was formed to carry out the first major European research work into social enterprise between 1996 and 1999 across the fifteen European Union countries and was later formed into the EMES International Research Network for the continuance of social enterprise research. As stated earlier, the Network is made up of university research centres and individual researchers whose goal is to develop the literature around social enterprise (EMES). A priority of the EMES approach very early on was to identify indicators to help define social enterprises. In doing so, it was not the intention to prescribe characteristics which were essential in order to be defined as a social enterprise, but rather, as a guiding framework for relating differing organisations which could be broadly construed as such within the field.

The EMES approach has been adopted by significant research bodies as a means of creating a working model for research into social enterprise, most notable of these is the Organisation for Economic Co-operation and Development (OECD) and Pearce in *Social Enterprise in Anytown* (2003). Similarly, the Labour government in the UK launched the Social Enterprise Unit in 2001 to establish and co-ordinate good practice in social enterprises. In the following year the government's social enterprise strategy, *Social Enterprise: A Strategy for Success* was launched (DTI,

2002). To further the aims of the government strategy, the Social Enterprise Coalition (SEC) was established with government funding (SEC, 2003). The Social Enterprise Coalition identifies three shared common characteristics of social enterprise which includes enterprise orientated, social purpose and social ownership. Similarly, Pearce (2003) identifies six defining characteristics of social enterprise which are: social purpose, engaged in trade, limited distribution of profits, assets held for community benefit, democratic governance and independence organisations.

The European Research Network (EMES) conceptual framework is based around indicators of social and economic criteria. Social enterprises, unlike the traditional non-profit organisations, are normally not engaged in advisory activities as a major goal or in the redistribution of financial flows (as, for example, grant-giving foundations). Instead, they are directly involved in the production of goods and the provision of services to people on a continuous basis. The provision of services represents, therefore, the reason, or one of the main reasons, for the existence of social enterprises (Nyssens, 2006). Social enterprises are voluntarily created by a group of people and are governed by them in the framework of an autonomous project. Although they may depend on public subsidies, public authorities or other organisations (federations, private firms, etc.) do not manage them, directly or indirectly. They also have the right of participation and to terminate the project (Nyssens, 2006). Those who establish a social enterprise assume totally or partly the risk of the initiative. Unlike most public institutions, their financial viability depends on the efforts of their members and workers to secure adequate resources (Nyssens, 2006). As in the case of most traditional non-profit associations, social enterprises may also combine monetary and non-monetary resources, voluntary and paid workers. However, the activity carried out in social enterprises requires a minimum level of paid workers (Nyssens, 2006). One of the principal aims of social enterprises is to serve the community or a specific group of people. To the same end, a feature of social enterprises is their desire to promote a sense of responsibility at local level (Nyssens, 2006). Social enterprises are the result of collective dynamics involving people belonging to a community or to a group that shares a certain need or aim. They must maintain this dimension in one form or another (Nyssens, 2006). Further, voting power is not distributed according to capital shares, the owners of capital are important, but the decision-making rights are shared with the other stakeholders (Nyssens, 2006). Representation and participation of customers, stakeholder orientation and a democratic management style are important characteristics of social enterprises. In many cases, one of the aims of social enterprises is to further democracy at local level through economic activity (Nyssens, 2006). Social enterprises not only include organisations that are characterised by a total non-distribution constraint, but also organisations like cooperatives in some countries, that may distribute profits only to a limited extent, thus avoiding profit-maximising behaviour (Nyssens, 2006).

The Organisation for Economic Co-operation and Development (OECD) identifies social enterprises as having an entrepreneurial approach in pursing both economic and social goals (2006). The OECD has identified a set of key elements which define social enterprises across its thirty member countries. These characteristics closely resemble the characteristics identified by the EMES Research Network and also encompass both economic and social criteria.

To explore the relationship between the four individuals/organisations research into social enterprise, the characteristics are summarised and discussed in further detail. The similarities and differences between the descriptions by the researchers are highlighted in Table 5.1.

Table 5.1 summarises the key characteristics of social enterprises according to SEC, Pearce, EMES and OECD. There is significant overlap in the characteristics identified by all the organisations and individuals but the first five are shared by all and are discussed further here. However, it

Table 5.1 Social enterprise key characteristics

Key characteristics	*SEC*	*Pearce*	*EMES*	*OECD*
Directly involved with trading activities	x	x	x	x
Social aim or purpose	x	x	x	x
Limited or non-distribution of profit/surplus	x	x	x	x
Participation and governance by stakeholders	x	x	x	x
Independent/autonomous organisations	x	x	x	x
Assets held for a social benefit		x		
Minimum amount of paid work			x	x
Initiative launched by citizens/stakeholders with shared aim			x	x
Decision-making powers not related to capital ownership			x	x
High level of economic risk			x	x

should be noted that although there is some consensus over the characteristics of social enterprise, it is only at a very abstract level (Young & Lecy, 2012). The exact meaning of social purpose, for example, has not been considered in these characterisations and furthermore, the different versions of social enterprise already considered such as social firms will have different priorities in relation to these characteristics when compared with a cooperative. This book will consider the meaning of social purpose in relation to the common good and virtues in the context of MacIntyre, which will provide for a level of practical understanding that is absent from the abstracted characteristics identified in Table 5.1. Furthermore, Pearce distinguishes between radical and reformist social enterprise, which will be detailed in later chapters towards creating a clear philosophy for social enterprise.

Directly Involved with Trading Activities

Social enterprises are engaged in some form of continuous trading or service provision to the market. This characteristic identifies the enterprise orientation of the organisation and is identified by all four organisations/individuals and is often cited as one of the primary goals. For example, the Social Enterprise Coalition refers to both enterprise orientation and social aims (SEC, 2003). Pearce subordinates the commercial role of the social enterprise as a means of achieving the social aim.

Social Aim or Purpose

Pearce (2003) argues that the social role of a social enterprise is the primary purpose. Indeed, all four theorists refer to this characteristic, which refer to the enterprise having a social purpose. The EMES and OECD definitions refer to aims which benefit the community, whereas the SEC refers to social enterprises having explicit social aims such as job creation or services to the community.

Limited Profit Distribution

It is useful to reiterate at this stage that social enterprises are profit or surplus making organisations, but their distribution differs to mainstream businesses. Social enterprises may have a system of limited profit distribution, or indeed, may prohibit the distribution of profits completely; for example, The McSence Group profits are reinvested and used to fund community needs such as a youth centre (Martin & Thompson, 2010). The primary aim of this characteristic is to ensure that social enterprises do not engage in profit-maximising behaviour. Profits are usually reinvested in the enterprise to maintain and promote the initiatives which support the organisation's social purpose. Indeed, this characteristic has the potential to ensure that a social enterprise is self-sustaining, if sufficient profits are reinvested through the organisation. The requirement to preserve both assets and profit/surplus for the benefit of the community further enhances the sustainability of the organisation. Indeed, in the UK, the legal framework for social enterprises is a Community Interest Company (CIC) which includes the legal requirement for an asset lock. This effectively ensures that the organisation retains profits or assets for the community benefit or for the social purpose of the enterprise because it is legally required to limit profit distribution.

Participation and Governance by Stakeholders

This characteristic identifies the stakeholder approach to management, in that all those affected by the organisation can participate or are represented in the decision-making process of the organisation. The OECD and EMES research refer to a democratic management style and Pearce refers to the democratic involvement of members in organisational governance. Participation and governance are linked to the EMES and OECD characteristic relating to capital ownership and decision-making, in that decision-making is not carried out by management as agents for shareholders.

Independent/Autonomous Organisations

Social enterprises are established by groups of people, or individuals, who have independently decided to address a social need. Thus, it is voluntary in nature and despite the potential for social enterprises to obtain government subsidies and grants, the individuals have the autonomy to operate the enterprise as an independent organisation and not be controlled by government decisions.

The research by the OECD identified the EMES contribution to the definition of social enterprise for the purposes of research. Initially, an entrepreneurial strategy and some form of social aim such as improving access to the labour market were determined as the common features of a social enterprise (OECD, 2006). However, this narrow definition has been expanded to incorporate additional elements relating to ownership, participation, community benefit and profit distribution criteria. The criteria or elements of the EMES definition are designed as indicators in recognising a social enterprise. This is primarily due to the diversity in the type of organisations which could be considered a social enterprise, for example cooperatives and social firms, to name only two. However, many of the defining characteristics can not only be ascribed to other types of organisations but are not always present in a social enterprise and therefore, not unique to social enterprise. Indeed, the only clearly defining characteristics according to Peattie and Morley (2008) are the primacy of social goals and the need to achieve them through trading. However, Defourny and Nyssens (2008) acknowledge the limitations of the EMES approach in that it is not an exact representation of reality, but merely a focus on certain features and a creation of emphasis for the purposes of research.

One of the key characteristics identified by all the organisations in Table 5.1 is the direct engagement with a trading activity, rather than merely as an advisory body or grant-giving organisation. It is not essential that the trading activity relates to the social purpose, merely that it trades with the intention or objective of pursuing or advancing the social goal. Young and Lecy (2012) point out that the EMES model does not provide for organisations outside of their ideal type and therefore excludes certain organisations which undertake socially beneficial activities, such as corporate social responsibility (CSR) programmes in traditional businesses. However, Kay et al. (2016) claim that such CSR programmes are a means of mitigating the impact of their behaviour. Whereas the characteristic model for social enterprise emphasises the primacy of social goals but equally requires the limited distribution of profit, which is incompatible with the traditional model of profit-maximising business. However, there is a school of thought (Alter, 2010; Dees, 1998) which supports the view that social enterprise can be placed on a spectrum which ranges from charitable organisations through to private companies. This is significant because social enterprises are being considered in a fundamentally different context to the ideal-type approach, if they are compared with, for example, private companies which maximise profit. The view held in this book is that social enterprises are fundamentally different from private and capitalist business because they are founded for a different purpose. The social enterprise is established to address a social need and only generates wealth for the purposes of continuing that social purpose. The social enterprise could be viewed as adhering to a rank order in which external goods in the form of wealth are subordinated to the internal goods and common goods of the enterprise. However, there are still some references to balancing priorities within the social enterprise literature which I will address in relation to the radical social enterprise later in the book.

Social Enterprise on a Spectrum

The Social enterprise spectrum theory asserts that a range of organisations have a combination of social purpose and profit orientation, which can all be considered when using the spectrum approach (Young & Lecy, 2012). Dees (1996, 1998) created a spectrum which identifies the key stakeholders and motives/methods and goals of organisations. The spectrum, according to Dees, has a range from purely philanthropic to purely commercial, depending on motives, methods and goals. For Dees, the focus of research is on the alternative approaches for funding in response to a decline in charitable and governmental funding and the drive towards for-profit activities of charitable organisations. Doherty et al. (2014) identify the growth in interest in social enterprise as being partly due to such developments. However, they also point out that a range of social, economic and political developments have created interest in social enterprise including new methods of delivering public services and an increase in alternative economic models to address inequality (Amin, 2009; Evers, 2005).

Alter (2010) expanded on Dees model to create more scope within the spectrum for alternative models such as social enterprise and CSR. Alter refers to a similar 'hybrid spectrum' in which the extremes are traditional non-profit and traditional for-profit, with social enterprise identified as a distinct section. Alter points out that organisations on the spectrum have different motives and priorities and align social enterprise with the left-hand side of the spectrum in which motive is related to the social mission, which in turn is determined by stakeholders. Whereas the right-hand side is driven by profit-making motives and distribution of profit to shareholders. Alter's spectrum indicates that social enterprise is focused on different priorities to the traditional for-profit entities, she identifies the different accountabilities for the two sides as being either stakeholder or shareholder. In many ways, Alter's spectrum can be viewed as two separate approaches to a social outcome, rather than a spectrum. A spectrum implies some continuum of ideas or methods, whereas I would argue that organisations from the profit-generating side of Alter's spectrum are fundamentally different in their accountability, motives and methods to the left side of his spectrum. Indeed, social enterprise is distinct for its mission motive, profit-generating abilities and stakeholder engagement from both traditional non-profit and traditional for-profit organisations (Pearce, 2003). However, Sasaki and Koizumi (2016) point out that despite the primary motive of for-profit corporations is to make profit, it can ultimately be related to a social purpose; it can therefore be related to a political and philosophical standpoint in that Neoliberalism promotes the capitalist accumulation of profit through economic development as a vehicle for social good. Their argument is a reflection of Adam Smith's, who also believed that individual pursuit of wealth would ultimately improve overall prosperity and the general good of society (MacIntyre, 2016). This viewpoint would support the inclusion of social enterprise within a spectrum as it is another means of creating social benefits. However, MacIntyre (2016) points out that Smith's argument fails to acknowledge that individual goods in economic activity can only be achieved through first cooperating to achieve common goods. Furthermore, the spectrum approach fails to create the hierarchy of internal and external goods and therefore does not fit with MacIntyre's rank ordering of goods because it encourages a balance between wealth creation and social purpose. The cooperative structure of social enterprises, combined with the social purpose is significant because combined they ensure that economic activities are directed towards the achievement of common goods (MacIntyre, 2016). Indeed, Pearce (2003) emphasises that a defining characteristic of social enterprises should be a cooperative structure, else not be deemed a social enterprise.

Young and Lecy (2012) claim that a spectrum aids in highlighting the idea of social enterprise and creates a useful metaphor which highlights that social enterprises have a range of both social and market-based goals, which can sometimes conflict or create tension. They describe the spectrum as a metaphor which does not impose rigid criteria and refers to key characteristics from the EMES type school of thought in which limited profit distribution and democratic governance could be dispensed with, making room for a greater variety of entities into its scope. However, Young and Lecy point out that such a metaphor does not clearly indicate where, if any, the boundaries are between private companies, social enterprise and non-profits. To incorporate such detail would move far away from the simplicity aimed for in the metaphor. More significantly, to remove the limited profit distribution as a requirement in the social enterprise criteria could risk losing the focus on the social aims. Indeed, Kay et al. (2016) suggest that maximising social rather than financial profit should be integral to the social enterprise and the indicator of their success. Furthermore, to ignore the importance of democratic governance in social enterprise is to undermine the significance of the power dynamic in the organisation; many social enterprises are based on the founding concept of mutuality such as cooperatives, credit unions, and employee-owned businesses. Indeed, all the organisations in the previous section identified 'participation and governance by stakeholders' as a key element in their characterisation of the social enterprise.

The focus in the spectrum approach relies on a 'catch all' approach which can include any type of organisation which has some form of social purpose. This is regardless of whether the organisation's social purpose has a priority over profit, is purely charitable, driven by corporate strategy or motivated by non-social objectives such as increasing market share. One of the aims of this research is to establish that social enterprise is fundamentally different from the organisations in the wider economy in that they are profit-making, whilst engaging in a social objective and thus, are neither charities nor private enterprises. Social enterprises, it will be argued, represent an organisational form which supports the common good, through its decision-making and ownership structure and social purpose, which will be elaborated using MacIntyre's work. Dobkin Hall (2013) views social enterprise as on a spectrum and sees its origins in welfare capitalism in which business leaders promote workers' welfare; corporate philanthropy such as Carnegie's approach in which wealth from industry should be used for its development and finally, corporate social responsibility (CSR). Thus, Dobkin Hall considers the historical roots of social enterprise to be in capitalist enterprises and cites examples such as Carnegie in creating an understanding of the role business plays in the social and political advancement of a society, not simply an economic role. However, such corporate philanthropy involves decisions on social benefits being determined by the owners of capital. Whereas social enterprises are run by individuals who combine to cooperatively decide their common good, based on social needs rather than capital ownership. Reflecting this approach is MacIntyre's (2016) argument that common goods must be determined before individual goods, for societies and communities to flourish. Dobkin Hall further elaborates that the origins of CSR can be related to social enterprise roots in that business leaders started to be concerned about working day length and productivity within their workforce, although this concern was primarily driven by demand for greater efficiency. For Dobkin Hall, the key factor in the origins of social enterprise lie in any efforts to combine 'doing well' financially with 'doing good' socially, which will therefore align with the spectrum theory in its broad approach. However, the emphasis is making employees and productivity more 'efficient' which is the antithesis of excellence necessary for individuals to engage in practices in accordance with MacIntyre (2007). Dobkin Hall takes a principally corporate view of the rise of social enterprise and does not consider the many alternative routes such as the cooperative movement, labour movements or indeed changing attitudes to political and community roles, such as the growth in devolved responsibility to communities to address social needs. A key element to understanding the core of social enterprise is to view its ideological position in terms of social versus economic; organisations with a corporate form will have an economic imperative which prioritises wealth and profit. Whereas social enterprise originates from the social imperative, which prioritises social benefits over profit. To appreciate this fully, social enterprise needs to be viewed in a wider context, giving due consideration to its historical antecedents. It is easier to appreciate the social imperative at the core of a social enterprise when viewed through the historical lens of labour and cooperative movements of the Industrial Revolution. Furthermore, social enterprise as a concept first appeared in Europe in 1990, firmly grounded within the third sector.

To summarise thus far, the social enterprise spectrum theory asserts that all organisations with some form of social outcome can be included in the spectrum, ranging from the purely philanthropic to corporate social responsibility activities in commercial enterprises. Dees (1998) developed the spectrum theory which was further elaborated by Alter (2010) to show a more nuanced breakdown of organisations within the spectrum. Social enterprise was aligned more towards the non-profit organisations in Alter's spectrum due to their motives being related to social mission, rather than profit motives associated with corporations on the other end of the spectrum. Dobkin Hall (2013) also views social enterprise on a spectrum and determines its origins are aligned with corporate philanthropy. However, this does not consider any other approaches other than a business orientation, in the evolution of social enterprise, for example, through the cooperative movement, labour movement and changing social and political attitudes. This distinction is important because the values and priorities will differ depending on the approach; a corporate approach will prioritise profit and wealth, whereas the labour movement will focus on the welfare of the workforce. I argue in this book that social enterprise viewed as part of a spectrum incorporating both extremes, fails to acknowledge its origins and its essence in which the social imperative is the priority with profit-making (rather than profit maximising) necessary only to the extent that it enables the organisation to continue to create social benefits.

Pearce (2003) identified six characteristics of social enterprise which have been incorporated in the section on key characteristics earlier in the chapter. His definition relies heavily on the six characteristics he has defined, with the social purpose being paramount. Furthermore, Pearce argues against individual gain in favour of collective benefits in his six characteristics. Furthermore, he views social enterprise within the wider economy in relation to private enterprise, public sector and third sector. The first system, or private is focused on profit and maximising returns to shareholders and ranges from micro-businesses through to multinational corporations. The second system is traditional known as the public sector and is responsible for the redistribution and planning in the economy through democratically elected institutions. The third system includes the family, neighbourhood and informal institutions through to the social economy in which social enterprise is situated. Pearce also identifies that social enterprises have a spectrum of their own whereby they range from a 'reformist' approach in which activity is seen as a supporting role for the private and public systems where they provide services that are not provided by the other systems; to a 'radical' approach in which social enterprise represents an alternative system to the existing dominance of the private system. The significance of the radical versus the reformist approach will be explored in the next chapter and how it can be related to MacIntyre. I argue that radical social enterprises can represent MacIntyre's view of a virtue embodying institution.

Conclusion

The approach to defining social enterprise adopted by EMES and the OECD provides a valuable insight into the characteristics of social enterprise. The characteristics identified by the individuals and organisations in this chapter suggest that social enterprise is different from both third system and first system organisations, in particular, the primacy of labour over capital in decision-making and operations and the importance of profit to further stakeholder interests, rather than shareholders. Nevertheless, there is some common ground; private sector in terms of making a profit and public sector in terms of meeting social needs. However, social enterprises exist in many forms and are unlikely to meet all the ideal criteria, particularly given the diversity of such organisations and their many forms.

The spectrum approach encompasses all organisations with some form of social activity, from the extremes of purely philanthropic to commercially focused profit-maximising enterprises. Social enterprise according to this theory is considered somewhere between the two extremes and more towards traditional non-profit organisations according to Alter (2010). Alter gives greater regard to motives and priorities in the organisation and considers who the organisation is accountable to in the spectrum. However, a spectrum implies a continuum of ideas and methods throughout its range which seems at odds with the differences in terms of the combination of accountability, mission motive and profit priorities associated with social enterprise. Despite there being some value in being able to highlight the basic idea of social enterprise in such a broad context, as pointed out by Young and Lecy, such categorisation may be harmful by misleading people into thinking social enterprise is a form of charity or commercial business. Whereas it is argued here that social enterprise is a fundamentally different type of organisation with different values and aims to both ends of the spectrum and as such should be considered as a radically different type of organisation which is a product of its values and its history. This view can be aligned with MacIntyre's hierarchical structuring of goods in which social enterprises also use such hierarchy to ensure the social purpose is paramount. However, the spectrum approach highlights the possibility for a balance or trade off to occur when determining what MacIntyre would term internal and external goods. Thus, a more radical form of social enterprise should be explored to determine the commitment to a rank order of goods. Pearce identified two alternative views of social enterprise, termed 'radical' and 'reformist'. The reformist social enterprise engages with the existing systems defined by Pearce as first/private system, second/public service system and third/self-help/charitable system and attempts to improve and reform it from within. The radical approach is more concerned with creating an alternative system to the first system of profit and wealth maximisation which would reflect the values of the third system.

References

Alter, K. (2010). *Social enterprise typology*. http://www.4lenses.org/setypology (Accessed 20 September 2016).

Amin, A. (2009). Extraordinarily ordinary: Working in the social economy. *Social Enterprise Journal, 5*, 30–49.

Borzaga, C., & Defourny, J. (Eds.). (2001). *The emergence of social enterprise*. Routledge.

Dees, G. (1996). *The social enterprise spectrum: Philanthropy to commerce*. Harvard Business School, Publishing Division.

Dees, G. (1998). Enterprising non-profits: What do you do when traditional sources of funding fall short? *Harvard Business Review, 76*(1), 54–67.

Defourny, J., & Beveltere, P. (1999). *The social economy: The worldwide making of a third sector*.

Defourny, J., & Nyssens, M. (2008). Social enterprise in Europe: Recent trends and developments. *Social Enterprise Journal, 4*(3), 202–228.

Dobkin Hall, P. (2013). Philanthropy and the social enterprise spectrum. In T. S. Lyons (Ed.), *Social entrepreneurship: How business can transform society*. Volume 2: Approaches to Financial Social Entrepreneurship. Praeger

Doherty, B., Foster, G., Mason, C., Meehan, K., Rotheroe, N., & Royce, M. (2009). *Management for social enterprise*. SAGE Publications Ltd.

Doherty, B., Haugh, H., & Lyon, F. (2014). Social enterprise as hybrid organisations: A review and research agenda. *International Journal of Management Reviews, 16*, 417–436.

ECOTEC: Research & Consulting Ltd. (2003). *Guidance on mapping social enterprise: Final report to the DTI social enterprise unit*.

EMES International Research Network. http://emes.net/index.php?id=203 (Accessed 14 February 2010).

Evers, A. (2005). Mixed welfare systems and hybrid organisations: Changes in the governance and provision of social services. *International Journal of Public Administration, 28*, 737–748.

Grant, S., & Dart, R. (2009). *The social construction of social enterprise*. EMES Conferences Selected Papers Series. Available at www.emes.net (Accessed 22 October 2010).

Henry, N., Johnson, T., & Spear, R. (2006). *Social enterprise: An international literature review*. GHK.

Kay, A., Roy, M. J., & Donaldson, C. (2016). Re-imagining social enterprise. *Social Enterprise Journal, 12*(2), 217–234.

Kerlin, J. (2006). Social enterprise in the United States and Europe: Understanding and learning from the differences. *VOLUNTAS: International Journal of Voluntary and Nonprofit Organizations, 17*(3), 246–262.

MacIntyre, A. (2007). *After virtue* (3rd ed.). University of Notre Dame Press.

MacIntyre, A. (2016). *Ethics in the conflicts of modernity: An essay on desire, practical reasoning and narrative*. Cambridge University Press.

Martin, F., & Thompson, M. (2010). *Social enterprise: Developing sustainable businesses*. Palgrave Macmillan.

Nyssens, M. (Ed.). (2006). *Social enterprise*. Routledge.

Organisation for Economic Co-operation and Development OECD. (2006). *The social enterprise sector: A conceptual framework*. OECD.

Pearce, J. (2003). *Social enterprise in Anytown*. Calouste Gulbenkian.

Peattie, K., & Morley, A. (2008). Eight paradoxes of the social enterprise research agenda. *Social Enterprise Journal, 4*(2), 91–107.

Sasaki, S., & Koizumi, M. (2016, June 28–July 1). *Elaborating upon the social enterprise spectrum through the perspective of ethical capitalism*. Paper submitted to the 12th International conference of the International Society for Third Sector Research, Ersta Sköndal University College, Stockholm, Sweden.

Social Enterprise Coalition. (2003). *There's more to business that you think: A guide to social enterprise*. Social Enterprise Coalition.

Spear, R., & Bidet, E. (2003). *The role of social enterprise in European labour markets*. European Research Network. https://emes.net/?id=203 (Accessed 22 March 2010).

Young, D. R. (1983). *If not for profit, for what? A behavioural theory of the nonprofit sector based on entrepreneurship*. Lexington Books.

Young, D. R., & Lecy, J. (2012). *Defining the universe of social enterprise: Competing metaphors* (Working Paper 12-25). Andrew Young School of Policy Studies Research Paper Series.

CHAPTER 6

Contextualising Pearce's Social Enterprise

Introduction

As noted in the previous chapter, Pearce (2003) situates social enterprise within the third system of the economy which includes voluntary organisations and the family economy. The distinction is important in relation to the previous chapter in which various modes of social enterprise were examined, including positioning social enterprise on a spectrum which included capitalist organisations engaged in some form of corporate social responsibility. However, this was viewed as contrary to MacIntyre's rank ordering of goods. Social enterprise within the third system of Pearce's theory distinguishes it from the capitalist first system and the second system of state responsibility. Pearce further distinguishes between reformist and radical social enterprises; in the reformist approach, social enterprises work in conjunction with the first and second systems, addressing social needs in communities where state assistance has been withdrawn and the first system cannot make sufficient profit. Reformist social enterprises have adopted several previously state managed responsibilities in relation to housing, social care and many other areas. Radical social enterprises are more political according to Pearce because they are attempting to create an alternative to the first system of private enterprise in which social needs are prioritised over capital accumulation. The distinction in relation to radical social enterprise is crucial because it can be clearly identified as distinct from the capitalist and

G. Hall, *Virtue and Social Enterprise*,
https://doi.org/10.1007/978-3-031-14027-3_6

private approach of the first system and demonstrates a rank ordering of goods. In this chapter, the third system, also referred to as the social economy is explored in greater detail to create a landscape for understanding social enterprise and the values that underpin such organisations. Radical and reformist social enterprises are discussed to highlight the distinction between them and create a framework to elaborate further on radical social enterprise. The social and political context will be considered to identify the influences on radical social enterprise and explore the implications of their existence and growth on the wider economy. Pearce only refers briefly to the radical form of social enterprise, which in my view, is the most appropriate form of social enterprise to reflect MacIntyre's virtue theory. Therefore, this chapter and the next will fully develop the characteristics of a radical social enterprise so that it can be analysed against MacIntyre. My view agrees with Pearce that the dominance of capitalism cannot be changed whilst also collaborating with it and thus, radical social enterprise is the focus in this work. Pearce describes social enterprise with both characteristics and values; the characteristics are similar to those identified by the EMES network and OECD, as discussed in the previous chapter. However, he elaborates on the characteristics with a set of values which form the basis for how social enterprises should operate but identifies that the values tend to lack clear focus and specific meaning. The intention is to elaborate on the values identified by Pearce with MacIntyre's work to impose clear meaning on the values. Pearce argues that social enterprises need to articulate their values and how they lead to positive, practical outcomes for a community. Moreover, social enterprises need to collaborate to build shared values through establishing networks which work together. I argue that MacIntyre's expression of virtues through practice embodying institutions can provide the practical meaning for the values of social enterprise provided that external goods are subordinated to internal goods.

The Social Economy

Pearce in his characterisation of the social economy and social enterprise created a circular diagram to identify their positioning within the overall economy (Fig. 6.1). There are three distinct sections to the diagram based on their key values; identified as first, second and third systems and within each system the different elements of the economy are identified: neighbourhood through local, national and international at the outer edge of the circle. The first system, or private system, is focused on capitalist profit and maximising returns to shareholders and ranges from micro-businesses through to multinational corporations. The second system is traditionally reflected in the public sector and is responsible for the redistribution and planning in the economy through democratically elected institutions. The third system includes the family, neighbourhood and informal institutions through to the social economy in which social enterprise is a part. Furthermore, according to Pearce, by placing social enterprise within the first system, one would fail to recognise the role and importance of the other elements within the third system and their importance to the running of the private and public systems. In particular, family, neighbourhoods, mutual assistance such as giving lifts and the numerous types of organisation within civic society such as social clubs (Pearce, 2003). Pearce points out that it is the first system which dominates most Western economies but suggests that if the third system were to be dominant, with first and second systems not removed but within a mixed economy, the values associated with the third system would influence the other systems and prevail over all the economy. The values to which, Pearce argues, organisations in the third system should subscribe are drawn from a set of 'value statements' established by The European Network for Economic Self-Help and Local Development. They include cooperation, decentralisation, inclusivity, good work, sustainability and people-centred. Pearce argues that all social enterprises should abide by these values because they are what distinguishes the third system from the first and second systems. Beyond the values, social enterprises are defined by characteristics such as social purpose, non-profit distributing and democracy (Pearce, 2003). The combination of social enterprise characteristics and values are what distinguish social enterprises from capitalist enterprises and government provision according to Pearce and as such, it is crucial that they are adopted as core to the organisational structure and purpose. For, without them, the social enterprise is in name only, and better fitted to the first or second systems. However, I argue in this book that the values which Pearce ascribes to social enterprises are too vague, indeed, Pearce also suggests that they are often expressed in vague terms such as 'working for the common good' and 'putting people before profit'. He suggests that the values need to be identifiable through a clear philosophy in which practical outcomes can be derived. It is my aim in this book to align MacIntyre's work on virtues and the common good with social enterprise to create such a clear philosophy. According to Defourny (2001), there has been a significant growth in initiatives which do not fit within either the for-profit sector (first system) or the public sector (second system). These organisations can be categorised within the third sector or social economy. The third sector is a relatively recent term associated with initiatives by charities, social enterprise, voluntary organisations and a range of other organisational types. According to Defourny, the term social economy is an historical concept which dates to the nineteenth century during the industrial revolution, when dramatic changes were occurring in the economic system.

The third sector has been described by Pearce (2003) as consisting of a number of elements, including social enterprises, voluntary organisations, charities and also family. This description locates social enterprise within the third sector or system, but also considers its separate role of profit-making activity which is distinct from the activity of family or charity. Pearce argues the values which underpin the social economy and are embedded in community led organisations and grass-roots institutions such as social enterprises are representative of a challenge to the prevailing values in the capitalist system. Furthermore, Pearce suggests that the social economy is the foundation and platform for the development of a civil society and central to civil society is the voluntary association by members of the society of which they are a member.

Social Enterprise as a Part of the Social Economy

Social enterprise as part of the social economy, rather than as a subset of the private economy or the public system, is an important distinction because it clearly identifies social enterprise as different from the private system of business. Thus, avoiding the potential for social enterprise to be viewed on a spectrum as detailed in the previous chapter in which corporate social responsibility and philanthropy are considered within the same spectrum as social enterprise. Pearce argues that social enterprises within the social economy are predicated on the values identified in the previous section which are crucial to the development of social enterprise as a virtuous organisation in accordance with MacIntyre. Kay et al. (2016) suggest that the neoliberal or free-market principles of economic society are being subject to increasing scrutiny because of the creation of inequality in wealth and power. They point out that social enterprise could represent a viable alternative to the existing dominant system of enterprise.

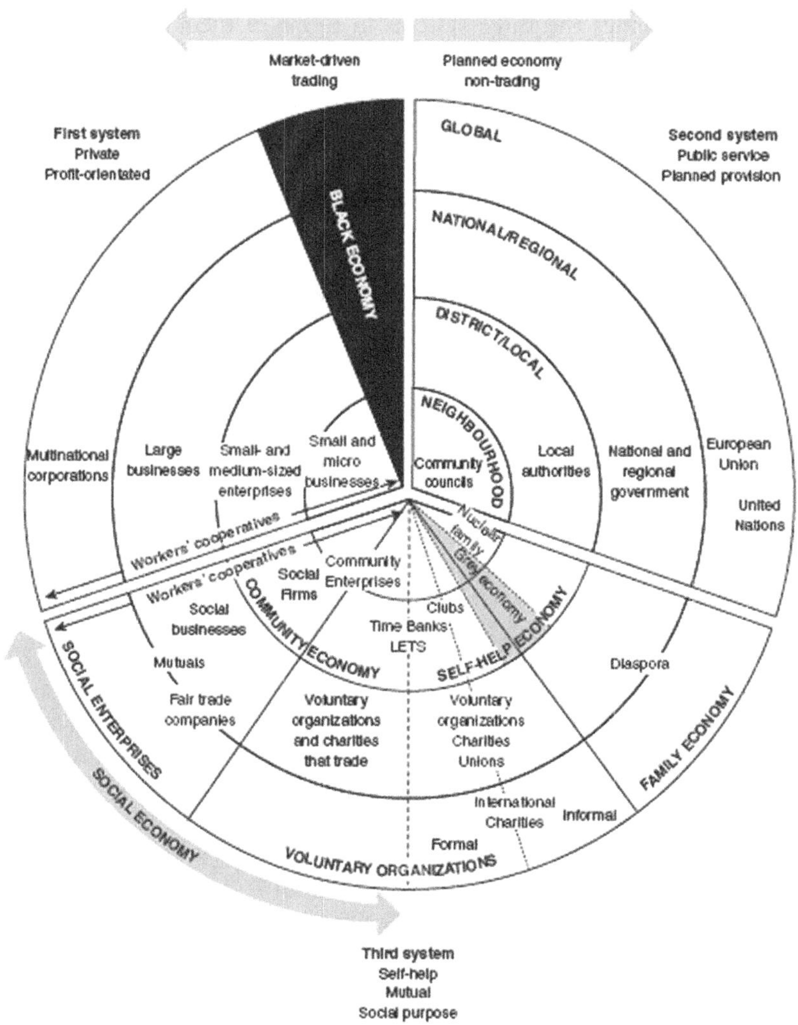

Fig. 6.1 Three systems of the economy (Pearce, 2003)

Pearce separates the three systems in terms of their values; with the first system being profit driven and focused on capitalist principles of shareholder wealth maximisation, which encourages and rewards individual wealth and profit maximisation, above all else. The second system in which government takes responsibility for determining and delivering public services. The third system is based on citizens determining their own needs through mutual support and focusing on social needs rather than profits. Pearce argues that social enterprise values would be at risk if they were deemed a subset of the private or public systems. They are at risk of being subsumed into the values and purposes of those systems because of the dominance of capitalism and government power (Pearce, 2003). Furthermore, social enterprises would risk moving away from a rank ordering of their goods towards a balanced approach which creates the potential for focusing on the external goods of wealth. For both Pearce and this book, the distinction is vital; the values specific to social enterprise form the foundation of what is essentially different and worthy of research because of the possibilities arising from an organisation which has a social purpose, supported by sufficient profits to sustain itself. In this book, I argue that social enterprise represents a virtuous alternative to the free-market system which dominates most Western societies in which cooperation and social goods are prioritised whilst profits are still achieved. However, the values in social enterprise need to have philosophical weight to give them a solid foundation. Currently, social enterprises are often viewed as businesses with a social agenda, which misses the fundamentally different role and structure that social enterprises could represent in society. MacIntyre provides a foundation for the purpose of social enterprise in his representations of the common good and its importance to the wellbeing of society and communities. Given a philosophical basis for their existence and purpose, social enterprises could be viewed as a viable alternative to the dominance of capitalism. The first system, it is argued, is founded on private ownership, individualism and profit orientation; whereas social enterprises are founded on common interests, shared ownership and a common good orientation. It is therefore argued that the current dominance of capitalism serves the interests of the owners of capital who accumulate wealth through profit-oriented organisations. The capitalist system encourages individualism at the expense of common interests according to MacIntyre (2016) to further the pursuit of wealth by the owners of capital and production. Thus, capitalism serves the owners of wealth through institutions which focus on efficient and effective methods of creating profits. Whereas, social enterprises are created by cooperative actions by community members to address a common interest. They operate through democratic decision-making based on shared interests, rather than capital investment and have aims which are oriented to a common good.

Central to Pearce's characterisation of social enterprise as within the social economy of the third system is the primacy of social purpose and social need. Where an organisation operates as a worker-based cooperative, if it does so for the maximisation of profit for its members, then it would be deemed part of the private system according to Pearce, because it does not have a social purpose as its main priority. Indeed, the achievement of profits is secondary and is seen as the means to achieving the primary social purpose (Pearce, 2003). The social purpose could be related to the local community, environmental needs, worker participation and a myriad of social concerns (Pearce, 2003). The engagement in trade characteristic could be achieved through varied means including income from goods or services direct to the public, government contracts to deliver public services, grants from public bodies, trusts or foundations, fundraising measures and voluntary labour (Pearce, 2003). Each of the methods of income generation presents different challenges; grant funding can limit the scope of the social enterprise through stipulations on its uses, government contracts can be viewed as a means to privatising previously government responsibilities in society. Related to this point are the characteristics of democratic involvement and autonomy; social enterprises must ensure that influence from large benefactors, or government contracts does not impact on the founding social purpose of the organisation or impede the democratic involvement of its members and the wider community. Social enterprises aim to achieve profits for reinvestment in the organisation, to further the social purpose for which it was established (Pearce, 2003). Their social purpose is to work for the common good according to Pearce, which is also a central focus in MacIntyre's approach and will be analysed in greater detail in the next chapter. Pearce argues against individual gain in favour of collective benefits. Similarly, MacIntyre (2016) argues that individual goods can only be achieved through first understanding our common goods through a shared understanding and deliberation of our common goods. The assets of the social enterprise are always held in trust for those which it exists to benefit, they are not available for individual gain; this is a distinguishing characteristic of the social enterprise which separates it from capitalist enterprise. The democratic involvement of members is also critical; this may be in relation to a local community or a group further afield. Regardless, it is essential that those affected by the organisation have a democratic right in decision-making and governance. Social enterprises adopt a 'labour employs capital' approach in which all members have a right to vote and contribute to the decision-making process. Pearce argues that democracy is a much deeper issue than simply 'one member - one vote' principle; he suggests that the third system is predicated on the belief that within civil society, of which the third system is representative, its institutions are the means for people to organise themselves. Pearce further suggests that the democratic practices of social enterprise can set an example in the wider political spectrum and encourage people to participate in their community. The last characteristic according to Pearce is accountability in relation to its members and wider society. Here the organisation is transparent in its activities and how it is managed so that it is clearly demonstrating its commitment to the social purpose and the democratic processes to achieve them, together with the values which underpin the organisation. It will be argued that the characteristics of social enterprise can be likened to MacIntyre's theory of an institution which encourages practices, through their commitment to the common good which is achieved through some form of trading process. They prioritise internal goods and subordinate external goods through the limited distribution of profits and common ownership features. Furthermore, they engage in a form of political behaviour through democratic decision-making which involves the wider community, is not based on capital ownership and encourages shared deliberation to ensure that common interests are pursued.

Pearce's characteristics distinguish social enterprises from the private system of business, he also identifies the values which underpin the social economy and therefore apply to social enterprises within it. They may not form part of any written constitution like the previous characteristics, but nevertheless, they represent the ethical basis for the third system according to Pearce. He bases the values on the European Network for Economic Self-Help and Local Development's value statements which form guidelines for organisations in the social economy and therefore, social enterprises. Whilst some of the values are encompassed in the characteristics already detailed, there remain six values which Pearce believes should be an inherent part of a social enterprise. These values include cooperation, decentralisation, inclusivity, good work, sustainability and people-centred. MacIntyre's views on the role of virtues and how they can be achieved through common goods and the development of practices could provide the philosophical underpinning to the values which Pearce espouses.

Values in Social Enterprise

The values in social enterprise include cooperation between organisations within the social economy to support each other rather than compete. Pearce points out that the third system is a substantial part of the overall system and thus, the value of *cooperation* between social enterprises can create significant advantages. MacIntyre considers cooperation as central to his view of practices (2007) and his view of the type of institution which could embody practices (2016) because it is essential to achieving the common good, as determined through shared deliberation towards determining common interests. The second value is *decentralisation* in terms of placing power in the hands of those at the lowest appropriate level (Pearce, 2003). Local communities should be in control of their own communities and only delegate upwards to a larger body or government should the need arise, whilst still retaining control, with the larger body remaining accountable to the community. Social enterprise could and should have a central role in ensuring such processes are created (Pearce, 2003). MacIntyre also believes in the importance of local democracy and views political society as a necessarily local or community process in which individuals combine to determine their common goods. Thirdly, *inclusivity* to ensure equal rights and opportunity to participate without discrimination of any kind, including race, gender, political belief or economic disadvantage; part of the role of social economy organisations is to respect the basic rights of people (Pearce, 2003). Similarly, MacIntyre (2016) argues that every argument and opinion is heard and given due weight in the process of making and sustaining local communities. Fourthly, *good work* in terms of both being socially useful in that it enhances the general quality of life for people or for a specific group, and enjoyable for those engaged in the organisation in relation to their work, conditions and rewards (Pearce, 2003). MacIntyre's description of a practice detailed in Chapter 2, takes the value of good work to a far more detailed and meaningful level to ensure that the workplace provides the opportunity to engage with practices towards achieving individual and common goods. The fifth value according to Pearce is ***sustainability*** which relates to both the organisation being able to maintain itself and sustainable work practices to preserve and protect the environment. Sustainability as a value can be likened to MacIntyre's flourishing communities, achieved through working towards the common good. However, this is a developing area of study in relation to how to create growth, without depleting the Earth's natural resources. The role of social enterprise in creating organisations which do not necessarily encourage economic growth and also measure growth through different means will be explored in greater detail later. Lastly, ***people-centred*** rather than capital-focused, social enterprise should ensure that success is measured in the social impact rather than financial outcomes. Capital is necessary to serve the social purpose but is not an end in itself; profit is necessary, only to the extent that it achieves the social purposes of the organisation. As noted in Chapter 2, MacIntyre would similarly argue that the internal goods of practices should be prioritised in the institution and external goods should be sufficient only to sustain the practices which are supported by the institution.

Kay et al. (2016) revisit Pearce's work and attempt to re-imagine it in a more up-to-date context from when it was written in 2003, suggesting that social enterprise could be a radical approach to creating organisations which reflect a fairer society. Pearce's approach aligns with the argument in this research that such a focus and understanding of common goods and the values inherent to social enterprise suggest that it is possible for them to be virtuous organisations. However, to determine whether social enterprises are virtuous requires a synthesis with MacIntyre's work which will be addressed in the next chapter. Furthermore, the view that communities can democratically create socially responsible solutions to their needs, links to MacIntyre's view that communities should be the source for creating common goods. Chakrabortty (2018) wrote for *The Guardian* newspaper, a series of articles which report on people and communities that are finding alternative economic approaches for social problems. He describes these examples as evidence of what a democratic and decentralised economy may look like. Throughout the articles, there are examples from across the UK of alternative approaches to capitalist business, through social enterprises and community action, with examples of what he describes as civic institutions including the Bevy in Brighton which is both a public house and a community centre. He also describes a growing number of social enterprises in Plymouth being established in response to social needs, ranging from a café which helps people with dementia to an arts centre which have been developed by local people with the support of the local community. Chakrabortty (2018) points out some common themes across these groups which include an appreciation of values, an opposition to the capitalist market measures of value, and participation in the community by individuals to provide for their own social needs.

Radical and Reformist Approaches

As noted throughout this book, Pearce also asserts that social enterprises have their own spectrum ranging from a 'reformist' approach in which activity is seen as a supporting role for the private and public systems where they provide services that are not provided by the other systems; to a 'radical' approach in which social enterprise represents an alternative system to the existing dominance of the private system. Ridley-Duff and Bull (2016) make a similar assertion in identifying two significantly different social enterprise approaches which align with Pearce's radical and reformist. Pearce argues that radical and reformist social enterprises are at opposite extremes—with the former being supportive of the first and second systems through helping to address the shortcomings of these systems, and the latter actively seeking ways of creating a viable alternative through a more political approach. Radical social enterprise is a political manifestation of finding an alternative approach and as such requires an embedded commitment to the values of the social enterprise that Pearce espouses. Whereas the reformist social enterprises are arguably colluding with the existing system by providing support where the private and state systems have withdrawn or provide inadequate investment in the social aspects of the economy and the wellbeing of society. Pearce argues that it is not possible to create meaningful change to the system whilst also supporting the existing system. I argue that radical social enterprises represent virtuous organisations which conforms with MacIntyre's view, because they work towards achieving the common good through democratic decision-making and they are not subject to the influences of capitalism in the same way that reformist social enterprise may be. According to Kay et al. (2016), reformist social enterprises are more susceptible to the private system approach than radical social enterprises, because their values are less focused on the core values of social purpose and consequently less committed to the rank ordering of goods. This is particularly so where social enterprises are competing with private business because they not only have to ensure a profit, but also a social profit which can become eroded in the challenge to compete with private system organisations which usually do not have this additional concern. They are effectively trying to compete in the mainstream marketplace with organisations which do not have to consider the social impact of their actions in the same way as the social enterprise. Similarly, the radical social enterprise will be established with a foundation of shared values and social purpose, but they too will be exposed to external pressures which threaten to compromise their objectives, which can potentially lead to them becoming more reformist in their approach (Kay et al., 2016).

Kay et al. (2016) argue that not all types of social enterprise are beneficial and can indeed be harmful to the social good. They suggest that in the UK, successive governments have encouraged social enterprises as a means to reducing expenditure on public services (Kay et al., 2016). The provision of public services by social enterprises risks their independence to achieve social goods, through political and governmental decisions. In particular, Kay et al. (2016) identify that governments focus on the outcomes of the social enterprise, rather than their shared values and how they operate. Clearly, there is the risk of compromise to the fundamental values of the social enterprise when all that is being measured or assessed are the outcomes. Added to this concern is the competitive environment in which social enterprises are being challenged by private businesses for the provision of previously public services. Social enterprises may compromise their values in order to compete with private business or risk being replaced. In short, the focus is not on how things are done, but on measuring the outcomes. Thus, losing the essence of social enterprise in how and why they operate.

Reformist social enterprises, according to Fitzhugh and Stevenson (2015) are attempting to change the way the private and public systems operate from within, suggesting that reformist social enterprises are less interested in definitions of what social enterprise is, and more focused on reducing the boundaries between social enterprise and private business. They propose that the infiltration of social enterprise ideas into the mainstream could increase the expectations on capitalist business to be more concerned for social outcomes. However, the capitalist system of private enterprise remains focused on the profit and wealth creation for its owners/shareholders. It is the radical social enterprise which represents an alternative economic system to the existing capitalist approach and could challenge capitalism's dominance. Pearce also defends the view that reformist social enterprises act as support to the existing capitalist system by providing goods and services in areas where the public system has withdrawn, and the private system could not make sufficient profit to encourage them to engage. Thus, reformist social enterprises may be viewed as enabling the first and second systems to focus on other priorities whilst it takes care of those areas in society which have suffered from the lack of state support or harmed by the first system of private gain. Whilst the social economy encompasses the range of social enterprises from radical to reformist, it is the radical which represents the alternative system.

Larner (2014) describes Coexist, which is a group of people who formed to create a community in Bristol, UK, providing work and creative opportunities for its participants. There is acknowledgement amongst Coexist according to Larner that they are actively seeking alternatives to capitalism whilst being run through a non-hierarchical management structure, with a cooperative ethos and a focus on creativity. Larner points out that, contrary to neoliberal approaches which focus on individual responsibility, Coexist focuses on collaboration, partnerships and community empowerment to achieve their goals. Originally the organisation did not fit within a designated organisational form, but clearly related to the social economy and social enterprise with its hybrid structure (Larner, 2014). Coexist is now registered as a community interest company and therefore acknowledges itself as a social enterprise. Larner points out that the terminology of social enterprise has been increasingly used since it was established in 2008 to describe their activities. Coexist, represents a working example of a radical social enterprise which prioritises the creative and focuses on cooperation and its ability to work towards the common good through collaboration and purposeful discussion and does not focus on profits or external goods as described by MacIntyre. Coexist was refused a new lease on the building (Hamilton House) which housed their activities because the owners wish to sell it. An offer from Coexist to purchase the building was rejected in favour of greater financial reward (Coexist Press Statement, 2018). The influence of the free market is felt on the radical social enterprise in this context and serves to highlight the difficulties faced in a market system dominated by capitalism. Kay et al. (2016) suggest that just as capitalism influences the norms and culture of society, so too could radical social enterprise in promoting equality, fairness and the common good. My aim is to provide the philosophical basis, through MacIntyre, for radical social enterprise to clearly identify as a virtuous organisation and recognise their contribution to the wider project of creating viable alternatives to the dominance of capitalism.

A Conceptual Framework for Radical Social Enterprise

Pearce views the radical approach as representing an alternative economic system based on shared values and primacy of people over capital. Kay et al. (2016), in reimagining Pearce's view of social enterprise, suggest that radical social enterprise uses economic activities as a means to an end, which is the social outcome as good; the economic activity is not therefore an end in itself; prosperity is related to wellbeing and the good of the community and not based on wealth or economic gain. I argue that radical social enterprises, as virtuous organisations are representative of non-economic prosperity and using MacIntyre's work, will identify the non-economic benefits of common and individual goods to be gained from such an organisation. Kay et al. (2016) further suggest that the prevailing culture in a society influences how people behave and point out the profound impact profit-based organisations from the private system have on the prevailing beliefs in society; such as the importance of competition and self-interest. Fitzhugh and Stevenson (2015) point out that radical social enterprises struggle more because they are grounded in collective action in a society based on individualism. According to Kay et al., the radical social enterprise can and should challenge the cultural norms of economic wealth taking primacy over social and societal values, through their overt application of values and adherence to them in the face of economic challenges such as competition from private, first system organisations. However, Chell et al. (2014) points out that social enterprises are not automatically ethical simply by their status of having a social purpose and pressure to conform to the existing economic system which prioritises wealth and profit can create pressure to moderate ethical values. Nevertheless, the aim for Kay et al. (2016) is to explore the possibilities for Pearce's radical social enterprise and suggest that they could represent a socially beneficial alternative to the existing economic system. The focus should be to use economic activity as a means to the ends of social, environmental and societal impact, thus shifting the focus from economic activity as an end in itself to a means to an end. Kay et al. also suggest a number of positive implications from their paradigm for social enterprise: social benefits would be a legitimate end; social enterprises could establish values for living and working together; and also the undertaking of activities which do not contribute economically but do create prosperity through exchange systems and linked to this is sustainability in terms of re-use of goods and alternative methods of exchange. Kay et al. are advocating for a hierarchical ordering of goods which ensures that common and internal goods are dominant over external goods.

The radical social enterprise represents a challenge to the existing capitalist system which dominates the economy of many western countries by presenting an alternative way of doing business which does not require the maximisation of profit, at the expense of social benefits. As noted earlier, Pearce points out that social enterprise values tend to be expressed in rather vague terms and suggests that a clear philosophy is needed for people to identify with and act upon. MacIntyre describes the need for virtues to achieve individual and common goods which, he argues, are ultimately needed for the wellbeing of communities. Pearce describes radical social enterprise as being an alternative to capitalism and its dominance in society. It is my aim to relate MacIntyre's virtue theory to radical social enterprise to create the clear philosophy Pearce suggests. Furthermore, democracy in social enterprise forms part of the wider democracy of the social economy in which all members of society can influence decisions through associations and organisations such as parent-teacher associations; it is not only national democracy in politics that has influence according to Pearce. Particularly where subsidiarity is involved in the democratic process, social enterprises can play a key role in ensuring that initiatives which affect their members are discussed and decided through discussion. MacIntyre would describe this as shared deliberation, which is necessary in determining common goods, which will be discussed in greater detail in the next chapter. Pearce considers that social enterprise has a political role which represents an alternative to the dominant first and second systems in which society is run according to shared values.

The Social, Economic and Political Context for Radical Social Enterprise

Radical social enterprise can be viewed within a larger framework of organisations and individuals that are attempting to radically alter the dominance of capitalism and free-market economics. According to Gibson-Graham and Roelvink (2011), there is a growing concern in the ability of the free-market economy to address environmental and social problems in society. High unemployment, climate change and reducing financial revenues are viewed as indicators of concern with the economics of capitalism. However, Gibson-Graham and Roelvink suggest that one of the main barriers to acceptance of alternatives is in our assumption, whether acknowledged or not, that capitalism is the only model available. Healy (2009) suggests that because the capitalist model is so powerful and dominant, it is difficult to view alternatives as anything other than idealistic, inferior and powerless. Gibson-Graham et al. (2013) suggest that the economy needs to be reframed as a process which all can engage with, rather than an impersonal system or machine which cannot be influenced to any great extent, suggesting that it is a key factor in influencing the social and political understanding towards new norms of thinking about the economy and the possible alternatives. There has been a growth in movements seeking to develop such alternative economies including the World Social Forum (WSF) and the Community Economies Collective (CEC). In particular, the CEC (2001) aims to encourage more sustainable development through new approaches to economics and politics. The CEC refers to the 'Community Economy' which emphasises the diversity of economies which exist that focus on alternatives to the financial imperative of capitalism. The community element refers to a democratic process of open collective negotiation. They emphasise that the economy is not a fixed system which cannot be altered or changed; it is not 'The economy' but rather economies or economic practices. The CEC has a strategy to expand the scope of discussion around the economy so that it is broader than the dominant capitalist understanding. Their aim is to create understanding of the diversity of economies which exist that are not based on the profit focus of the capitalist model. Gibson-Graham (2006) argues that capitalism is presented as dominant and immovable, thus making it difficult to envisage alternatives. They suggest that non-capitalist forms of economy should be conceptualised and represented to reduce the belief in capitalism's unassailable position.

The World Social Forum was established in 2001 in opposition to the domination of capital, neoliberalism and imperialism. The forum seeks, through debate, to find alternatives to the global influence of capitalism's multinational corporations and the governments which serve their corporate interests (World Social Forum, 2018). Further, they consider issues such as democracy include creating an enabling environment for civil society organisations and alternative forms of democracy such as participatory democracy. The forum is held annually with participants including Universite du Quebec a Montreal and the World Fair Trade Organisation. Gibson-Graham (2006) suggests the World Social Forum is one movement which has helped to create academic and political interest in economic alternatives to capitalism. The Solidarity Economy is a term that has emerged in the 1980s to refer to economic activities which do not prioritise profit but instead promote quality of life within communities (Safri et al., 2016). The focus for the organisations within the solidarity economy is democratic control and collective decision-making and includes organisations that constitute social enterprises, such as credit unions and cooperatives. Indeed, according to the Solidarity Economy Association, the values are mostly drawn from the cooperative movement, but require a more proactive approach to inclusive democracy and self-management than traditional consumer cooperatives (www.solidarityeconomy.coop/). The solidarity economy has roots in the social economy, particularly in Europe in attempting to address social and economic disadvantage (Miller, 2006). However, it has grown into a movement through research and activity and like the CEC, aims to create recognition that the economy is not a fixed capitalist system, but instead, a mixture of diverse economies. Similar to Pearce's depiction of the three systems of the economy, the solidarity economy recognises the wealth of existing economies within what Pearce would largely deem to be the third system, of networks of families, community groups and social enterprises which embody the values of solidarity, cooperation, democracy and subsidiarity. Kawano (2018) suggests that the solidarity economy provides a framework for guidance, rather than a set of rules, which include economic behaviour which is in accord with the values of solidarity, equity and participatory democracy. Bollier (2011) refers to a 'commons paradigm' in describing the social practices of organisations in civil society which work together to create collective benefits. The commons generally refer to resources which belong to or affect the whole community but when viewed in economic terms, researchers are developing the concept towards finding alternative forms of wealth creation to the typical western capitalist model and use it to refer to a focus on community or common good, rather than individual good. MacIntyre's virtue theory develops the virtues through practices with the purpose of creating flourishing communities. Similarly, Pearce refers to sustainability as one of the values of social enterprise. Bollier (2011) describes the diversity of the commons from the traditional understanding of land, to internet developments such as open-source software. 'Commoning' describes the organisation and practice of commonly participating in an activity which meet a common need and emphasise common objectives and a democratic decision-making process. An example of the link between commoning and social enterprise are community gardens which are run by local people in a sustainable way using previously unused land for the benefit of the community, usually through volunteers who benefit from the garden's produce. This type of community garden could fit the characteristics and values of a social enterprise in accordance with Pearce. Kay et al. (2016) identify the growth in the social and solidarity economy (SSE) in which mutuality and localism are promoted through volunteering, a focus on livelihood rather than jobs and the retention of local assets to benefit the community. They suggest that the impetus for this movement is in Latin America but suggest that the SSE could be crucial in helping to overcome the dominance of capitalism through a focus on localism, both socially and economically.

Social enterprise and particularly radical social enterprise represent an alternative to the capitalist model which can be aligned with these theories of diverse economies. They suggest that there are a diverse range of transactions and exchange methods which take place, including alternative methods to money in goods and services exchanges, alternative ways of carrying out labour and methods of remuneration which can create prosperity and wellbeing, without involving the financial economy (Kay et al., 2016). Radical social enterprise can be viewed as utilising many forms of transactions and exchanges, for instance, the use of voluntary labour or the circular economy in which material goods are exchanged and recycled. Pearce viewed community economic development as challenging the dominant capitalist structure, and organisations such as social enterprises as the means to testing alternative economic structures. The political ideology for an economics of the common good is different to the dominant ideology of liberal markets and wealth accumulation, but that is not to say that it is not a viable alternative. Indeed, the view from within social enterprise is that they could have transformative possibilities (Hayday cited in Fitzhugh and Stevenson, 2015). Fitzhugh and Stevenson (2015) observe that many people involved in social enterprise believe that it could have a significant impact on first sector businesses. However, Hayday (2015), like Pearce, suggests that social enterprise should be the alternative, rather than a supplement to the mainstream of private business. However, Fitzhugh and Stevenson (2015) identify that political debate and narrative around social enterprise mostly focus on its usefulness, whereas the focus should be on the social context, power balance and democratic participation. They point out that groups such as EMES identify with the wider political and philosophical issues such as participatory governance, but there needs to be greater political discussion around the nature of social enterprise as a movement. Furthermore, many of the interviewees in their research from within social enterprise, identify with both the reformist view of achieving their specific goals within a community and also with the broader, radical role that social enterprises can play in changing the economy. Pearce (2003) clearly argues that social enterprises cannot be both supportive of the existing system whilst also trying to replace it. Therefore, it is important to determine the role of social enterprise in society, which can then be clearly articulated, promoted and further researched. A clearly defined purpose for radical social enterprise can be determined through the application of MacIntyre's approach to the role of common goods in society. According to MacIntyre, common goods are essential to our understanding of individual goods and it is only through first identifying those common goods that we begin to understand our own goods. The aim here is to articulate how radical social enterprises achieve common goods through their activities and structure, giving them a clear role in society which is also a viable alternative to capitalism.

Conclusion

Pearce (2003) positions social enterprise with the social economy and third system of the economy, thus promoting the view that social enterprises are not part of the private system on a spectrum as discussed in the previous chapter, but rather, are part of a system which is based on values such as the common good, local economy and democratic involvement. Pearce elaborates on the characteristics and values which should form the foundation of a social enterprise but points out the lack of a clear philosophy to support it and for people to engage with. The characteristics and values have been briefly likened to MacIntyre's virtue theory in particular the rank ordering of goods in social enterprise, but will be fully discussed in the next chapter. Pearce suggests that the social economy is the foundation of a civil society, supported by Defourny (2001), who points to a renewed interest in civil society since the financial crash of 2008 and increased awareness of global consumption and sustainability. This is further supported by the movements such as Community Economy Collective, the World Social Forum and the paradigm of the commons, which identify with a need to address economic issues in society, particularly in relation to sustainability and wealth creation. Pearce's radical social enterprise represents part of these movements through a rejection of the free-market system of capitalism, in favour of the common good being served by profits and wealth. Pearce considered the values of cooperation, subsidiarity, democratic decision-making and good work should be core to an organisation's work to ensure there is no drift towards capitalist behaviour. It is argued here that radical social enterprise represents an alternative economic system based on shared values and primacy of people over capital. Together with movements which emphasise the common over individual good, radical social enterprises provide an alternative which is already in existence and not a theoretical model which has no practical evidence to assess whether or not it is viable. Pearce points out that the first and second systems are important but should not be dominant. In the next chapter, radical social enterprise will be fully developed to describe a social enterprise that is consistent with MacIntyre's virtue embodying institution, which will be synthesised with MacIntyre's work on the virtues as an alternative to the dominance of the free market, based on common interests.

References

Bollier, D. (2011). The growth of the commons paradigm. In C. Hess & E. Ostrom (Eds.), *Understanding knowledge as a commons: From theory to practice* (pp. 27–40). The MIT Press.

Chakrabortty, A. (2018, September 26). Yes, there is an alternative. These people have shown how to 'take back control'. *The Guardian*. Available at: https://www.theguardian.com/commentisfree/2018/sep/26/alternatives-take-back-control-local-projects-austerity (Accessed 28 September 2018).

Chell, E., Spence, L. J., Perrini, F., & Harris, J. D. (2014). Social entrepreneurship and business ethics: Does social equal ethical? *Journal of Business Ethics, 133*, 619–625.

Communities Economies Collective. (2001). Imagining and enacting noncapitalist futures. *Socialist Review, 28*(3–4), 93–135. http://www.communityeconomies.org/key-ideas (Accessed 19 September 2018).

Defourny, J. (2001). Introduction: From third sector to social enterprise. In *The emergence of social enterprise*. Routledge.

Fitzhugh, H., & Stevenson, N. (2015). *Inside social enterprise: Looking to the future*. Polity Press.

Gibson-Graham, J. K. (2006). *The end of capitalism (as we knew it): A feminist critique of political economy*. University of Minnesota Press.

Gibson-Graham, J. K., Cameron, J., & Healy, S. (2013). *Take back the economy: An ethical guide for transforming our communities*. University of Minnesota Press.

Gibson-Graham, J. K., & Roelvink, G. (2011). The nitty gritty of creating alternative economies. *Social Alternatives, 30*(1), 29–33.

Healy, S. (2009). Economies, alternative. In R. Kitchin & N. Thrift (Eds.), *International encyclopedia of human geography* (Vol. 3, pp. 338–344). Elsevier.

Kawano, E. (2018). *Seven ways to build the solidarity economy*. https://www.opendemocracy.net/en/transformation/seven-ways-to-build-solidarity-eco nomy/ (Accessed 15 January 2019).

Kay, A., Roy, M. J., & Donaldson, C. (2016). Re-imagining social enterprise. *Social Enterprise Journal, 12*(2), 217–234.

Larner, W. (2014). The limits of post-politics: Rethinking radical social enterprise. In, J. Wilson & E. Swyngedouw (Eds.), *The post-political and its discontents: Spaces of depoliticisation, spectres of radical politics*. Edinburgh University Press.

MacIntyre, A. (2007). *After virtue* (3rd ed.). University of Notre Dame Press.

MacIntyre, A. (2016). *Ethics in the conflicts of modernity: An essay on desire, practical reasoning and narrative*. Cambridge University Press.

Miller, E. (2006). Other economies are possible! Organizing toward an economy of cooperation and solidarity. *Dollars & Sense: The Magazine of Economic Justice*. http://socialeconomyaz.org/ (Accessed 10 May 2017).

Pearce, J. (2003). *Social enterprise in Anytown*. Calouste Gulbenkian.

Ridley-Duff, R., & Bull, M. (2016). *Understanding social enterprise: Theory and practice* (2nd ed.). Sage.

Safri, M., Healy, S., Borowiak, C., & Pavlovskaya, M. (2016). Putting the solidarity economy on the map. *Journal of Design Studies, 9*(1), 71–83.

Solidarity Economy Association. www.solidarityeconomy.coop/ (Accessed 12 November 2018).

World Social Forum. (2018). https://fsm2016.org/en/sinformer/axes-themat iques-2016/ (Accessed 24 September 2018).

CHAPTER 7

Radical Social Enterprise and MacIntyre

Introduction

This chapter will consider MacIntyre's work directly alongside Pearce's conception of social enterprise. The radical form of social enterprise is fully developed in this chapter, based on Pearce's original definition of a general social enterprise and his definition of radical, as distinct from reformist. As presented and detailed in the previous chapter, Pearce identified characteristics and values for social enterprise, which will be considered in the context of MacIntyre. Through a synthesis of the literature cited in the previous chapters, themes have been identified which are common to both Pearce and MacIntyre, this chapter will explore the compatibility of MacIntyre's work with radical social enterprise. The common themes identified are common goods, cooperation, democracy and rejection of capitalism which form core elements to the work of both authors. It is through the common themes and radical social enterprise characteristics and values that the rank ordering of goods is highlighted, to ensure that external goods are subordinated to common goods and internal goods. It is argued that radical social enterprise uses a hierarchy like MacIntyre to ensure that their social purpose is achieved. Radical social enterprises are identified and situated with the social enterprise field and within a broad outline of MacIntyre's work. The aim of exploring these common themes is to highlight the relationship between MacIntyre and radical social enterprise, together with empirical evidence

G. Hall, *Virtue and Social Enterprise*,
https://doi.org/10.1007/978-3-031-14027-3_7

from Coexist that demonstrate a commitment to common goods and putting community above profit, cooperation and creating an alternative to capitalism. Rejection of capitalism is fundamental to the radical social enterprise and is what identifies it as different from reformist social enterprise as described in the previous chapter. Radical social enterprises are attempting to create viable alternatives to capitalism as a market system and do not seek to reform capitalist and state organisations to address failings in society. Instead, radical social enterprises take a different approach in which external goods (as understood by MacIntyre) are used as a means to achieving common goods, rather than allowing external goods to dictate the role of practices and common goods in the institution. MacIntyre (1999) also argues that capitalism is at odds with his conception of how the virtues can be developed and should be rejected in favour of networks of giving and receiving as identified in Chapter 2. Furthermore, the culture in societies which support capitalism encourages individualism, which is at odds with his view that common goods must be understood as prior to individual goods in that we must first understand our common goods before we can begin to consider individual goods. MacIntyre considers common goods as key to achieving the virtues because qualities such as prudence, courage and justice are essential in the pursuit of common goods. Radical social enterprises support the social needs of a community and attempt to develop the common good through addressing those social needs, whilst demonstrating an alternative method of operating to capitalism. Shared deliberation is vital to ensuring that individual goods do not become the focus in discussions on how to achieve common goods. Radical social enterprises are committed to common goods through their social purpose. Indeed, it is the reason for the foundation of a social enterprise which was explored in greater detail in the previous two chapters (Pearce, 2003). MacIntyre (2016) argues that where individuals come together to address areas where common goods are lacking in their community, they are taking on a political role. Radical social enterprises play a role in that they encourage participation in community and society towards that end. Further, they can act as a catalyst for other organisations to adopt their approach and support those organisations in their efforts. Indeed, one of the important functions of radical social enterprise is to demonstrate an alternative approach to capitalism for society (Pearce, 2003). Cooperation is identified by MacIntyre as an essential element of practices and he uses examples of cooperative organisations to demonstrate the virtues and common goods. The values which Pearce asserts in social enterprise include cooperation and it is a vital element in achieving their social purpose. Moreover, democracy has an important function in both MacIntyre's and Pearce's work. MacIntyre argues that it is essential to the common good and the virtues and he views local communities as being suited to creating political communities in which individuals can deliberate together to determine their common goods. He argues that an intermediate area between family and state is necessary for such deliberation (MacIntyre, 1999) which, it is argued here, radical social enterprise can contribute to. Pearce sees social enterprise as having a role to play in local democracy and he argued that subsidiarity is the surest means of addressing the needs of a community. Radical social enterprises can play an important role in mobilising people to participate in their community through engagement with the radical social enterprise. The purpose of the synthesis of MacIntyre and Pearce is to demonstrate the compatibility of MacIntyre's philosophical thought with radical social enterprise. Radical social enterprise can be aligned with MacIntyre's view that goods have a hierarchy in which external goods are subordinate. They are also committed to maintaining the hierarchy in which social purpose is foremost, unlike business organisations which may seek to balance external and internal goods, therefore implying a trade-off and a weaker commitment to common goods and internal goods. This can provide the philosophical underpinning to the values that Pearce (2003) espouses in social enterprise, which he argues are too vague. The creation of a philosophical underpinning to radical social enterprise, therefore, can create greater validity for this type of organisation, whilst providing a source of theoretical study and model-building for radical social enterprise development. In short, MacIntyre uses cooperatives as institutions to demonstrate the creation of common goods and the development of virtues; applying his approach to radical social enterprises provides a much broader scope for application of his work, whilst demonstrating and philosophically defending a type of institution which also rejects capitalism.

Pearce (2003) identifies that radical social enterprises are part of an alternative approach which aims to create radical change to the political economy and society. Whereas reformist social enterprises are viewed as aiding the existing capitalist system through engaging in activities that are needed in society but are not sufficiently profitable for private enterprise to want to undertake, which is explored in more detail in Chapter 6. Radical social enterprises according to Pearce represent an alternative system of economic activity to the existing dominance of the capitalist system. Unlike their reformist counterparts which focus on supporting or mitigating the activities identified in the capitalist system through their social purpose, radical social enterprises attempt to create alternative methods of economic exchange and trade through their social purpose, detailed in Chapter 6 (Kay et al., 2016). Radical social enterprises are run for a social purpose which contributes to the common good of the community, using democratic decision-making methods through cooperation and common ownership. They acknowledge the interdependence of community members and create spaces where individuals can work towards their individual goods through an understanding of their common goods, which reflects MacIntyre's views on the importance of common goods and acknowledged dependence detailed in Chapter 2. Decisions are made through democratic processes in which workers or members of the social enterprise cooperate in their deliberations on the matters important to the community. The defining elements of a social enterprise have already been discussed in Chapters 5 and 6, but it is worth noting again that at their core is a social purpose. Common ownership is also critical in which all assets and wealth are held in trust for the continuation of the social purpose, for example the community. Democratic structures are also a key attribute whereby members can control the organisation. Pearce argues that democracy is essential to social enterprises because they are part of a wider democratic process in which communities organise themselves. Beyond the defining elements of social enterprises are their values of cooperation, collaboration, inclusiveness and democratic decision-making. Pearce includes local economy activities such as Local Exchange Trading Systems (LETS) and time banks as part of social enterprise. These types of activities enable people to contribute to the community through alternative exchange methods such as barter or time credits. Such an alternative form of exchange enables people to contribute in non-financial ways, which recognises the multitude of ways people can play a part in community.

The shared values of cooperation, collaboration, inclusiveness and democratic decision-making (Kay et al., 2016) will be aligned with MacIntyre's view of 'just generosity' and 'acknowledged dependence' in the radical social enterprise approach to create a philosophical argument for the role of radical social enterprise in developing a society which nurtures all contributions, whether economic or otherwise. According to Defourny et al. (2014), social enterprise can be viewed as a counterdiscourse to the existing neoliberal view of economic society in which communities can flourish, without needing to create economic growth. The understanding of common good is, therefore, fundamental to social enterprise activities through their social purpose, which creates an environment in which individuals understand their goods as being reliant on the achievement of common goods. Pearce also argues that social enterprises engage in a wider democratic process through their involvement in civil society. Furthermore, Pearce argues that social enterprises are part of practising democracy from the 'bottom up' so that people have direct control over their community. It will be argued here that radical social enterprises contribute to attempts to form local political communities and can provide the focus or lead in such attempts. They are, therefore, radical in the MacIntyrean sense in that their participants promote the idea of a wider and locally political common good. The enterprise can be considered ethically radical through democratic membership and decision-making in which individuals can pursue the 'internal goods' of their particular kind of productive work. The enterprise or institution can also be deemed politically radical where it fosters other, similar institutions in its locale. Coexist has encouraged a number of initiatives including the Community Kitchen, CoResist and the Bristol Bike Project and has been studied in detail by Larner (2014) over a three-year period. MacIntyre asserts that a group of individuals who think systematically about how their community can flourish through families, schools and workplaces and how their common goods can be achieved are essentially being political. MacIntyre elaborates on the requirements for a politics of local community which are shared deliberation with a common understanding and agreement on the interests of the community and how they can be achieved, together with democratic decision-making in which everyone has a voice, irrespective of power or ownership (MacIntyre, 2016). MacIntyre (1999) also refers to the virtue of 'acknowledged dependence' whereby individuals understand that throughout a lifetime, there are times where one relies on others and also times when others rely on us for their flourishing. Radical social enterprises acknowledge our inter-relatedness through social purpose and the democratic ownership and decision-making structure, which will also be discussed further in this chapter.

The previous chapters have discussed MacIntyre's virtue ethics and Pearce's social enterprise with the purpose of creating a philosophical basis to support radical social enterprise. An analysis of the key themes from MacIntyre and Pearce suggests a similarity in such aspects as cooperation, democracy, social or common goods and a rejection of capitalism. These themes together with the social enterprise values and characteristics will be considered in greater detail to support the synthesis of radical social enterprise with MacIntyre's work.

Social Enterprise Values and Characteristics

The values and characteristics identified as crucial to social enterprise were discussed in detail in the previous chapter and will be considered in relation to MacIntyre's work here. The overriding characteristic of social enterprise is a social purpose whilst trading to achieve that social outcome. Their purpose is not primarily to run a business, only to provide sufficient income to continue the social purpose, thus aligning with MacIntyre's view that external goods are subordinate to common goods and internal goods. Pearce argues that social enterprises contribute to the common good through their activities and aim to benefit society. MacIntyre asserts that common goods are necessary for us to determine our individual goods. There can be no conception of what our individual goods are, until our common goods have been determined. He argues that a political society is needed to understand and order the common goods in a society which is made up of individuals who are affected by such common concerns as family, education and workplace (MacIntyre, 2016). Social enterprises are established by concerned members of communities who wish to address a social ill. This is done through trading to ensure that sufficient income is received to sustain the enterprise. Similarly, MacIntyre argues that a practice embodying institution would focus on the practice and internal goods, whilst only requiring sufficient external goods to sustain the institution. Social enterprises prioritise the common good through their social purpose and only focus on external goods to the extent necessary to sustain the institution, with profits and assets held in trust by the organisation for the continuation of the social purpose. MacIntyre considers cooperatives as a type of organisation which can demonstrate a commitment to internal goods and practices, rather than external goods. He uses cooperatives to demonstrate the understanding of common goods in relation to individual goods and how they cooperate to achieve their common ends. Cooperatives demonstrate the democratic process of shared deliberation towards determining common goods, as do social enterprises in the characteristic of democracy, according to Pearce. He argues that open membership and a democratic structure are essential characteristics for a social enterprise. Indeed, Pearce argues that democracy is a much deeper issue than simply 'one member -one vote' and extends to engagement with democracy and politics whereby communities are encouraged to participate in organising themselves towards a flourishing society. Pearce argues that social enterprises play an important role in setting an example of the democratic process and encouraging people to participate. In this respect, social enterprise can be seen as contributing to the making and sustaining of local political communities in MacIntyrean terms. Particularly given that another characteristic of social enterprise is accountability, according to Pearce, in which the organisation is accountable to its members and the wider community in relation to its social purpose and how it is achieved. Beyond the characteristics, Pearce identifies a value base which is drawn from the third system of the economy where common interests, shared ownership and common goods are the focus. This is contrasted to the private ownership—individualism and profit-oriented—first system that is associated with capitalism. The values, according to Pearce, are cooperation, decentralisation, inclusivity, good work, sustainability and people-centred. These values can be assimilated with MacIntyre in relation to practices, goods and politics. Social enterprises should cooperate for mutual benefit and support according to Pearce but there is little mention of the cooperation within social enterprises beyond the common ownership characteristic previously detailed. An emphasis on cooperation within the organisation as well as with other social enterprises would aid in making clear that social enterprises are organisations that further the common good through cooperative actions. Furthermore, cooperation with the community and between individuals should be emphasised to demonstrate the commitment to shared deliberation and the common good which are features of the social enterprise. MacIntyre identifies the Thorupstrand cooperative as an example of a commitment to the practice of fishing, through which the common good and individual virtues can be developed which was detailed in Chapter 2. Similarly, social enterprises display cooperation and shared deliberation through their structure and decision-making processes and a commitment to the common good through their social purpose. Pearce argues that decentralisation is a core value for social enterprise, whereby local communities are able to organise themselves and respond to local needs. Decentralisation, according to Pearce, is essential to local democracy because it empowers local people and communities. MacIntyre argues that a political society is essential to the understanding and commitment to common goods which are required for a flourishing community as detailed in Chapter 2. He asserts that people need to have common concerns relating to family, schools and workplace so that shared deliberation can occur where there is largely agreement on the goods at stake and a shared conception of how such goods should be achieved (MacIntyre, 2016). Social enterprises play a role in encouraging individuals to engage in community activities which contribute to the common good. Through the value of inclusivity identified by Pearce, all people, without discrimination of any kind, should have an equal right and opportunity to participate in the activities which social enterprises undertake. Thus, contributing to the making and sustaining of local communities and reflecting MacIntyre in ensuring that every relevant voice is heard and not based on power and influence (2016). Pearce describes good work as another essential value for social enterprise, which he defines as work which is 'socially useful', enjoyable with good working conditions and fair remuneration. The good work value, therefore, relates to both the social purpose and the treatment of those working, volunteering or participating in the organisation. The introduction of MacIntyre's practice to the value of good work creates a far clearer role for the social enterprise in relation to its purpose and its activities. The articulation of social enterprise activities as practices would allow for recognition of the internal goods being achieved through the pursuit of common goods, defined through the social purpose. Social enterprises do not focus on external goods because they are driven by a social purpose, rather than the pursuit of wealth. It is, therefore, logical to determine that the activities carried out by those participating in the social enterprise can be deemed as engaging in a practice in which individual and common goods are the goal. The Community Kitchen at Coexist represents an example where the Kitchen is the institution in which the focal practice is cooking with a number of ancillary services which could also be deemed practices. The good and goal which all the practitioners are pursuing is a common one in encouraging the community to eat, learn and socialise and it is through an appreciation of the common goods associated with the shared experience of the kitchen that individuals acquire their internal goods. Furthermore, as the practices in the Community Kitchen are developed, the greater the benefit to the community through the kitchen's activities. Pearce (2003) refers to the value of sustainability as both relating to the future viability of the social enterprise and to ensuring that its activities are not harmful to the environment through its use of resources. The social enterprise protects its future viability through assets being held in trust but in relation to environmental sustainability, there are no clear guidelines. However, there is an increasing amount of research into how growth and prosperity can be measured without using the traditional economic approach. For example, Jackson (2017) elaborates on an alternative to the prevailing view that prosperity relies on material consumption and economic growth, in which people can flourish through social cohesion and improved wellbeing whilst consuming less. However, social enterprises form part of research into viable alternatives to capitalism which are sustainable and focus on flourishing communities, because of their social purpose and potential to be a sustainable alternative to capitalism (CUSP, 2019). The last value that Pearce identifies is people-centred, in which the priority for social enterprise is people rather than capital. How well the organisation performs is measured by the social impact, rather than level of profit as in capitalist business. Pearce argues that profits are to serve the interests of the people and should not be to their detriment. My view is that social enterprises are the embodiment of MacIntyre's view of an institution which develops the virtues through its commitment to social purpose and its achievement through a democratic structure, cooperative behaviour and by not focusing excessively on external goods. As an institution, a social enterprise bears all the elements which MacIntyre considers necessary for a practice embodying institution which encourages the virtues.

Key Themes

Rejection of Capitalism

MacIntyre has maintained a criticism of capitalism throughout his work; the virtues he defends are at risk from the individualism, acquisitiveness which focuses on external goods, to the detriment of internal and common goods which is discussed in depth in Chapter 2. MacIntyre (2007) argues that the values of the modern economic system are at odds with his conception of the virtues and that market values spread beyond the market system into non-economic areas of society, thus impacting on the virtues in a much wider context. He argues that the political and social structures needed to support the common good require a rejection of capitalism in its existing form (MacIntyre, 1999). The institutions which support communities with common goods as the priority do not promote economic growth, in favour of economic activity which support networks of giving and receiving in which goods are genuinely common.

MacIntyre argues that institutions and communities working towards common goods and developing networks of giving and receiving, are pursuing alternative measures of success to the recognised economic measures of capitalism. MacIntyre considers the view of academic economists that such communities are threatened by the free market because they impede growth and therefore, should be more economically efficient to succeed. However, MacIntyre (2016) observes that the cooperative fishing community of Thorupstrand, which is discussed in Chapter 2, are able to survive whilst concerning themselves with the flourishing of their community and subordinating economic outcomes to this end. Similarly, social enterprises focus on their social objectives and use economic means to achieve those 'other' ends. The performance of a social enterprise is, therefore, not measured in terms of increased wealth to owners and shareholders like capitalist business. It is measured by the social impact on the primary social purpose for which the enterprise was established (Kay et al., 2016). Any wealth generated through the social goals is held in trust for the future sustainability of the organisation and its future social goals. Furthermore, Pearce identifies that the role of capital in social enterprise is different to capitalist organisations in which labour and people are employed for the generation of more capital and asserts what he sees as the radical alternative of the primacy of people over capital. The radical social enterprise, therefore, for Pearce, seeks to subvert the free-market system of capitalism and bring about radical change to create a system based on their values, such as cooperation, democracy and primacy of people over capital. Indeed, Pearce refers to radical social enterprise as the 'stalking horse' in developing what he defines as a more political stance towards the economy, based on such values. It is important to note that Pearce's research originated in the predecessors of social enterprise, in cooperatives and community economic development. It is in this context that he describes community economic development as a political idea in which communities are run at a local level based on the pursuit of common goods. In addition, he refers to the development of community and cooperative organisations as not simply local projects to resolve local problems, but as attempts to create alternatives to the existing organisational forms which are based on cooperation, mutuality and limited wealth distribution.

Following from Pearce's analysis, social enterprises are structured to avoid the accumulation of wealth by individuals. So (as mentioned in earlier chapters), in the UK a legal form known as the Community Interest Company has been created which legally requires an 'asset lock' which prevents the use of capital for anything other than the social purpose and development of the social enterprise. Kay et al. (2016), in developing Pearce's work, refer to a growing disillusionment with free-market principles associated with capitalism, particularly since the financial crisis of 2008 and see radical social enterprises as representing an alternative to capitalism. Kay et al. (2016) in re-imagining Pearce's radical social enterprise create an alternative conceptual framework to the traditional view of a triple bottom line in social enterprise in which economic, social and environmental factors are all considered in the performance and outcomes of an organisation. Instead, they remove the economic element as an end 'in itself' and only as a means to achieving the social outcomes of the organisation (Kay et al., 2016). Thus, reinforcing the point that external goods are the lowest in the hierarchy of goods. They identify that prosperity in radical social enterprise is not based on profit and wealth for its own sake and instead a means to creating wellbeing for individuals and communities. Thus, further articulating Pearce's argument that all social enterprises should contribute to creating and developing a culture that promotes the common good (Kay et al., 2016; Pearce, 2003). Pearce and Kay et al. are effectively arguing, similar to MacIntyre, for a rejection of the capitalist values of individual gain, which encroach on all areas of society in favour of a culture of support and inclusiveness, essentially the virtues that MacIntyre espouses and as will be explored in more detail below.

More specifically, MacIntyre (2016) refers to cooperatives as institutions which support the achievement of common goods and argues that they are at odds with the dominant culture (of capitalism) because they challenge its morals and politics as discussed in Chapter 2. MacIntyre refers to the standard terminology of academic economics as measuring the value of contributions in work and society in monetary terms which are determined by the market. Whereas MacIntyre's measure of contribution relates to the common good and how institutions contribute to the development of understanding the individual's role in relation to the common good. For MacIntyre, it is essential that individuals develop a sense of their ability to contribute to the common good, rather than develop skills which will primarily serve to encourage economic growth.

In referencing the fishing community of Thorupstrand, MacIntyre is identifying the cooperative as a type of institution which is supportive of the community and its common goods. MacIntyre identifies Thorupstrand because of their commitment to the virtues of prudence in their political and economic actions, temperateness by not succumbing to the financial rewards of the free market, justice in the establishment of the cooperative and courage in taking appropriate risks to enable the cooperative to succeed. In a social enterprise, the primary purpose is social and aims to create a benefit to a community or a specific group. Moreover, in radical social enterprise, the focus is on the common goods which have been identified by the participants, the methods of deliberation to determine the common goods and the democratic structure of the institution will be discussed in greater detail within the themes in this chapter. The radical social enterprise, it is argued here, is established to create an environment which focuses on the needs of the community in which it is established, with a specific intent to subvert the economic goals of capitalism through demonstrating an alternative form of operating. They represent an alternative to capitalism, where people can create work which is fulfilling and generates sufficient income, whilst fostering the understanding of one's wider role and responsibility towards society in which the participants accept that they need to achieve the goods they have in common, before being able to achieve their individual goods. This creates a network of giving and receiving in accordance with MacIntyre which contribute to the common goods in the community. Larner (2014) points out that those engaged in activities at Coexist, do so with an understanding that they are pursuing an alternative to capitalism. The activities hosted by Coexist are not simply to meet financial needs, but to create opportunities for development, such as learning cookery in the Community Kitchen or CoResist a collective of artists who develop performance and workshops. The point here is that if MacIntyre's philosophical understanding of virtues and how they can be achieved is applied to radical social enterprise, it creates a much clearer understanding in terms of an alternative to capitalism in which individuals understand the value of common goods and cooperation in creating networks which create flourishing communities. The participants in Coexist see their role as more than a workplace, rather it is a means through which they can develop their own individual goods *and* the goods they have in common with their community. The emphasis is on common goods because of the nature of the organisation being a social enterprise which focuses on the social needs of the local community and the goods that are common to it. MacIntyre refers to the fishing crew of Thorupstrand in which their work is their way of life, rather than a means to external ends such as financial rewards. The fishing community, similar to Coexist, recognise that sustaining their way of life is an end in itself and resists the capitalist focus on individualism, in favour of community goods (MacIntyre, 2016).

Common Goods

MacIntyre argues that common goods are fundamental to the virtues in the context of practices, institutions and communities (Knight, 1998; MacIntyre, 2007, 2016). It is through the pursuit of common goods that we come to understand our individual goods, which can be achieved with a commitment to the virtues (MacIntyre, 2016). MacIntyre claims that the common goods of a community can only be determined through shared understanding and deliberation between members of a community, which is necessary to counter the bias of individuals towards achieving their individual goods. According to MacIntyre (2016), such bias towards individualism can be explained through capitalism encouraging society, through advertising and marketing, to consume products which do not contribute to human flourishing but rather, contribute to the expansion of capitalism through ever-increasing production. MacIntyre suggests those individuals who are concerned about their community and the common goods of family, school and workplace as taking a political role in society. For a politics of local community to function in the interests of a flourishing community, MacIntyre determines that democracy is essential to human flourishing and small communities are best suited to creating an environment which enables shared deliberation and democratic participation in the process.

As explored above in relation to Pearce, the institutional structure of the radical social enterprise encourages participation and discussion of how common goods can be achieved, through the pursuit of a common social purpose (Pearce, 2003). According to Pearce's analysis of social enterprise in general, the radical social enterprise, aside from the rejection of capitalism explored in the section above, should be founded on certain principles. These principles require the organisation to have a democratic structure which enables all those with an interest to have an input to the decision-making whilst being able to hold the organisation to account if decisions are not upheld. Pearce supports the devolved power to those at the grassroots of a community to emphasise the importance of local responsibility and accountability for the social impact of the organisation. Pearce also argues for the importance of 'human-scale' activity to ensure that local needs are at the heart of the social purpose. The radical social enterprise is founded for a social purpose which should work towards the common good of the community and ensure that external goods such as wealth are subordinate to this. Radical social enterprise can be viewed as an organisation which rejects the large-scale economy of capitalism by focusing on local methods of improving the local community, which are run with a democratic structure in which all participants are given the opportunity to have a vote and share in deliberations on the social purpose and how it will be achieved. Kay et al. (2016) argue that the solution to ensuring goods and services are allocated fairly and benefit society is by taking a 'local' approach.

In accordance with MacIntyre as explored here, radical social enterprises operate on a small scale in communities and respond to the needs of that community. MacIntyre (1999) argues that local communities are able, through shared deliberation and just generosity to foster the achievement of common goods through networks of giving and receiving. For example, Coexist develops their work in response to the needs of their community, through cooperation with the community members and the participants in the social enterprise (Larner, 2014). They also encourage the development of new social enterprises in response to the needs of the community, such as Coexist Community Kitchen which was established to develop cooking skills and provide an outreach to vulnerable groups in the community (Larner, 2014). As such, radical social enterprises are promoting the idea of a wider common good and contribute to attempts to form local political communities. They can also provide an example to others on how to establish organisations which contribute to the common good and provide support for developing social enterprises. For example, this was achieved through Hamilton House, which Coexist hosted to support other members of the community to establish socially useful activities which would benefit the community. Hamilton House provided a hub for activities to be developed by the local community, such as health and wellbeing courses and artists workshops which would all contribute to the community, supported by Coexist.

Following from the above description of Coexist, MacIntyre (2016) also explores how virtues are developed in certain types of institutions where practices and internal goods are prioritised over external goods which were discussed in detail in Chapter 2. Similarly, radical social enterprise is founded on its social purpose and views profits as a means to continuing the social purpose, rather than providing wealth to shareholders. It is concerned with the practices which develop the common good in a community; much like MacIntyre's view that economic activity should be directed towards common goods. MacIntyre also highlights that institutions which provide for common goods are characteristically in the form of cooperative enterprises. The suggestion here is that radical social enterprises share the characteristics of an organisation which can provide for common goods and represent a broader range of organisations than cooperatives, to which MacIntyre's views of virtue can be applied. Pearce (2003) states that social enterprises should contribute to the common good through their social purpose. MacIntyre explores the relationship between practices and institutions in which the practice with its internal and common goods is vulnerable to the behaviour of the institution. The acquisitiveness of the institution can subvert the practice and common goods and therefore, MacIntyre argues, the virtues of, including, justice, courage and truthfulness are essential to ensure this is avoided. Furthermore, MacIntyre argues that to exercise the virtues requires a sense of political and social engagement which acknowledges the interdependence of individuals, rather than simply as a series of individuals, each pursuing their own interests. He argues that institutions can encourage the virtues where there are enough individuals who are committed to these virtues and, moreover, understand the interrelatedness of individuals in a community. It is argued here that radical social enterprises are established primarily by such individuals who understand that they are developing an alternative form of organisation in which common goods can be achieved through collaboration and a cooperative organisational structure. Larner (2014) identifies Coexist as an organisation which is committed to creating an alternative to a capitalist organisation where individuals support each other through skill sharing and collaboration, towards achieving a common purpose of wellbeing in their community. They attempt to address the social deficiencies in their community as a means of addressing the imbalance of self-interest encouraged by capitalist influence in society (Larner, 2014). Radical social enterprises are established by groups of individuals who convene to deliberate on the social ills of a community and determine ways of remedying those ills. The cooperative and democratic structure enables shared deliberation on the needs of the community in accordance with MacIntyre

(2016). It is in this context that Pearce argues that radical social enterprises directly challenge capitalism by attempting to introduce a political economy based on values such as cooperation, collaboration, inclusiveness and democracy (Kay et al., 2016), which conflict with the liberal individualism that MacIntyre (2007) argues are dominant in today's society. Kay et al. (2016) similarly argue that radical social enterprises are a means for people to collaborate in creating greater equality and fairness, through different methods of exchange and service provision whilst contributing to the social good. Consistent with this analysis, MacIntyre asserts a key difference in how efficiency and growth are measured between cooperatives and free-market economics. He argues that academic economists view alternatives to the free market such as the Thorupstrand cooperative as inefficient and if they are struggling to survive, it is because they are inefficient in economic terms. However, MacIntyre (2016) suggests that what is at issue is how efficiency and growth are measured, which differs between the free market and cooperatives communities; the difference is about the ends to be achieved, rather than the means to achieving them. MacIntyre deduces that which ends are pursued depends on the virtues and vices of the people involved, arguing that those involved in the Thorupstrand cooperative demonstrated a commitment to the virtues of courage, prudence, justice and temperateness. Similarly, those individuals who establish radical social enterprises such as Coexist can be viewed as displaying the virtues of courage, prudence and temperateness. In short, they both share a commitment to a social good which benefits the community through shared deliberation and democratic decision-making and are also committed to an alternative form of economic engagement which rejects capitalism.

However, MacIntyre (1999) also suggests that to fully develop the virtues for a common good, an appreciation of acknowledged dependence is necessary. Whereby individuals realise that throughout life there are times when we are dependent on others for the achievement of our goods and at other times, we can also be responsible for others achieving their goods. MacIntyre argues that networks of giving and receiving are a necessary means to ensuring that such interdependence can be achieved. The radical social enterprise can be viewed as creating networks of giving and receiving through its social purpose and commitment to inclusiveness in the community. The commitment to the common good demonstrated in radical social enterprises reflects the understanding of our interdependence. MacIntyre (1999) determines that networks of giving and receiving can be institutionalised and suggests that such institutions would need to engage in shared deliberation, which is also a feature of the radical social enterprise. MacIntyre argues that an 'intermediate area' between family and the nation-state is where such networks of giving and receiving can be created. Radical social enterprises, through their commitment to a social purpose, explicitly presuppose a shared common good which determines the focus of shared deliberations, which is again consistent with MacIntyre's position.

A radical social enterprise such as Coexist represents an institution which encourages the development of networks of giving and receiving through the variety of activities they encourage. Larner (2014) describes Coexist as encouraging alternative types of lives and working environments because they encourage the development of socially beneficial activities in the local community. She also identifies that participants in the various activities are supported in learning together, all towards the core purpose of the social enterprise of supporting the common goods of the community. MacIntyre (2016) argues that community cooperatives such as Thorupstrand value their way of life which is supported by fishing. Coexist has a similar purpose in their activities, whereby their aim as an organisation is to build a way of life which values community and common good. Further, MacIntyre (1999) argues that the common good and its understanding rely on economic matters being subordinated to social considerations. There can be no significant inequalities in wealth if networks of giving and receiving are to be sustained. Radical social enterprises are run with a flat hierarchy and without the significant pay differentials between senior management and lower level workers, which are found in capitalist enterprises. Larner identifies that the directors of Coexist only accept a minimum living wage for their work and the organisation relies heavily on voluntary labour. The decision-making process at Coexist involves all participants and interested parties to ensure that activities and ventures benefit the local community, without being subject to the influences of capital ownership (Larner, 2014). Radical social enterprises use economic benefits as a means to achieve their social end and do not have shareholders with a capital interest to influence decisions. Capital is used only as a means to creating socially beneficial outcomes, rather than creating wealth for its own sake. In short, we might say then that MacIntyre argues that common goods need to be understood and achieved before it is possible to achieve individual goods; radical social enterprises embody the pursuit of cooperatively achieving common goods.

Cooperation

MacIntyre (2007) in his description of a practice suggests cooperation between people as essential to achieving excellence in their chosen activity, indeed it forms part of his definition of a practice which was detailed in Chapter 2. For MacIntyre, practices enable individuals to develop the virtues through cooperation with others. Common goods are linked to individual goods which can only be acquired through cooperation according to MacIntyre. MacIntyre (2016) views cooperatives as being institutions which encourage a commitment to common goods through practices. Furthermore, MacIntyre argues that common goods in relation to economic activities should be cooperatively achieved. The radical social enterprise can be considered as an enterprise which deliberately focuses its economic activity on the common good through cooperation. Both radical and reformist social enterprises, according to Pearce's definition, can be considered as cooperatives in which there is limited or no hierarchy and decision-making processes which enable all persons to influence decisions, regardless of their position. In radical social enterprises, there are shared values of cooperation, collaboration, inclusiveness and democratic decision-making which form the foundation for how they operate (Kay et al., 2016). Pearce identified the predecessor of social enterprise as community economic development, which he argued was a political idea which sought to show that communities and economies should be driven by the common good, rather than individual gain. He suggested that social enterprises continue this tradition of finding alternative organisational models which encourage democracy and cooperation. Thus, radical social enterprises in Pearce's view are economic institutions, founded on cooperative principles for the purposes of achieving the common good. MacIntyre (2016) cites cooperatives such as Thorupstrand and those established in Monte Azul which enabled common goods to be achieved through a focus on cooperation and shared deliberation. Radical social enterprises share MacIntyre's commitment to cooperation whilst also encouraging diverse activities to achieve their common goods, such as those provided at Coexist through the Community Kitchen, CoResist and Bristol Bike Project, all of which are ventures supported by Coexist to develop the common goods of the community.

Consistent with the above analysis, MacIntyre (2016) makes clear that virtues are evident in cooperatives; he asserts that the Thorupstrand cooperative demonstrated prudence, justice, courage and temperateness in their actions to ensure their success. Similarly, radical social enterprises can demonstrate such qualities in their rejection of the capitalist pursuit of profit and wealth, in preference for common goods of community which benefit all, whilst representing an alternative to the dominant economic systems of capitalism, which is both economically viable and just. Ballard (2000) argues that cooperatives, particularly Mondragon, which is a system of cooperatives, can demonstrate support for practices and internal goods. Pearce elaborates on a fictional town called 'Anytown' in which a variety of social enterprises are created to address the different needs of the community, all of which are run using the values of social enterprise to ensure the common goods of the community are met. Similarly, Emilia-Romagna in Italy has a thriving cooperative sector which delivers all goods and services, from groceries to health care. These examples demonstrate that cooperative activity, in accordance with MacIntyre's views on the virtues, can create economic institutions which contribute to the common good. However, the argument here is that radical social enterprise represents the most appropriate example of cooperation towards the common good because of its explicit rejection of capitalism and active pursuance of an alternative. First, Pearce advocates for a mutual model becoming dominant over the capitalist model of enterprise which, as MacIntyre asserts, the latter creates individualist acquisitiveness through the capitalist system. Second, the cooperative movement, argues Pearce, was aimed at creating opportunities for all people and to enable people to support each other in improving their lives. He cites Robert Owen in suggesting that a social system should not be based on self-interest but on mutual cooperation (Pearce, 2003). Third, the cooperative ethos, therefore, in line with Owen's view is that individual interest is not a sound principle for creating a social system, but rather, mutual cooperation can create a social system which works towards a common good.

Following the above analysis, the radical social enterprise represents the radical change that Pearce argues is needed to replace the capitalism model because of the commitment to cooperation for the common good. In radical social enterprises, cooperation reinforces the commitment to ensuring that capital ownership does not determine the priorities of the organisation. Radical social enterprises are established with a social purpose which is aimed at a common good for the community and as such, deliberate with those affected in the community about how to achieve their common good. Cooperation amongst all individuals is essential in the organisation to ensure that activities create the improvements necessary to create such a good. The ownership model for radical social enterprises is cooperative in that its assets and wealth are held in trust for the benefit of the community in the present and the future. The cooperative structure also embodies democratic ownership in which workers are able to control their own work which is important in MacIntyre's view of practices developing the virtues. The cooperative structure in radical social enterprises differs to capitalist business organisations because assets and accumulated wealth are held in trust for the benefit of the social purpose (Pearce, 2003).

Democracy

Democracy has three elements in both MacIntyre's and Pearce's work because of the political, social and economic implications of their ideas. MacIntyre (2016) argues for a politics of local community, whilst Pearce (2003) views social enterprises as part of local democracy. Both MacIntyre's and Pearce's work develop a view of society in which the common good in local communities is prioritised over the economic gain associated with capitalism. Furthermore, MacIntyre (2016) considers a political society necessary for individuals to develop the virtues needed for their individual and common goods. He argues that in modern society where individuals are concerned about the quality of their workplaces, education of their children and how they contribute to the common good, they are demonstrating political concerns. He suggests that even with single issues such as housing or education in a particular community, when common goods of the community are the focus, it is also a political society issue. Thus, where individuals attempt to develop a political society based on an underlying appreciation that their individual goods can only be achieved through the pursuit of common goods, they are creating a political society in which the virtues are able to flourish. Similarly, Pearce views social enterprise as having a political purpose which involves a different way of operating in society whereby people work for the common good. As previously explored, he argues for a radical change from capitalist liberal markets to alternative forms of organisation based on democracy and cooperation as a political idea, in which movements such as social enterprise and its predecessor, community economic development, operate as the political frameworks for an alternative to capitalism. He further argues that fundamental change is more likely in radical social enterprises because they do not support capitalism, unlike reformist social enterprise, but instead promote shared values that fundamentally challenge the pursuit of private gain (Pearce, 2003).

However, Pearce also accepts that promoting shared values is a rather vague term to describe the approach needed for radical change. In response to this issue, the argument defended here is that his aims in relation to community, capitalism and the common good are remarkably similar to MacIntyre's, and therefore can be underpinned by a more explicit and specific definition of shared values than Pearce gives, by applying MacIntyre's analysis to the practices of radical social enterprises as understood by Pearce. In other words, Pearce's shared values can be developed *in relation to* MacIntyre, in which individuals working in radical social enterprises understand the meaning and significance of the common good and its primacy over their individual goods (as defined by MacIntyre), else, we might assume, that they would not be involved in the radical social enterprise. In addition, within radical social enterprises, there is an implicit understanding of the need for cooperation and shared deliberation towards achieving shared goals for an improved community and society. The radical social enterprise, therefore, gives an institutional structure to the articulation of the ideas and strategies which work towards achieving the common goods identified through such a process. More specifically, MacIntyre (2016) determines key elements which are necessary for the achievement of common goods; shared deliberation assumes that there is some agreement on the goods at stake in their deliberations, which are in the interests of the local community. Also, that agreement can be reached or there is a shared conception of how the goods that have been agreed should be achieved. This should be done without prejudice or favour to any individual, ensuring that every relevant voice is listened to and all arguments are given due weight and attention. Power and influence are, therefore, not influencing factors in such decision-making (MacIntyre, 2016). Pearce determines that social enterprises democratically involve members of its constituency in decision-making and governance. He argues that radical social enterprises operate with values such as collaboration, inclusiveness and democratic decision-making. Pearce further asserts that social enterprises should have a democratic membership structure which enables all interests to participate in the decision-making process. Furthermore, he argues, social enterprises play a role in which members of a community can engage in the broader democratic process, to organise themselves for an improved society. He claims that social enterprises can set an example of a functioning democracy and encourage people to participate. According to Pearce, then, where social enterprises play a significant role in the redevelopment of a community, they can act as a catalyst to the creation of more development and regeneration. Similarly, MacIntyre (2016) uses small-scale communities to demonstrate the powers of local communities to develop the common good through politically democratic processes. Pearce, too, argues that social enterprises are 'at the heart' of the process of subsidiarity in which local communities are able to democratically manage their own affairs, contributing to the pursuit of the common good.

In summary, social enterprises can be viewed as economic democracies in which labour and the community have control over democratic decision-making, rather than capital ownership determining decisions as in capitalist organisations. Furthermore, Pearce suggests that community participation in social enterprises can encourage engagement with the wider democratic process, arguably enabling individuals to have a greater appreciation of their political role in society and how to achieve their common goods. Pearce, I believe, concurs with MacIntyre in arguing that democracy should not be something done by governments but should be part of all levels of society. Following from the above analysis, and consistent with MacIntyre's articulation of shared values as related to common goods, social enterprises are part of a democratic movement which enables people to democratically organise themselves for their common good. Pearce argues that for local democracy to work it needs to be developed and supported to ensure that people can participate in a meaningful way. In short, radical social enterprises can be held up as examples of functioning democracies which encourage people to participate in the democratic process, and as reflecting MacIntyre's understanding of shared values. This rank ordering of goods to ensure common goods are the primary good through promoting human flourishing within communities; served by internal goods related to specific practices of excellence and their associated virtues; which, in turn, are served by external goods such wealth creation. With the latter, therefore, only being promoted as a means to the end of the higher goods found in internal goods and common goods.

Radical Social Enterprises as Promoters of Social Purpose

As was established in Chapter 5, there is consensus of opinion that social enterprises are established for a social purpose such as creating employment for the long-term unemployed, training and employment for people who have a disability and services to a community such as community cafes (Pearce, 2003). However, radical social enterprises whilst attending to a social purpose also identify themselves as distinct from the capitalist system and seek to demonstrate a viable alternative to this system. Kay et al. (2016) emphasise that individual self-interest is not the driving force in social enterprise, but rather it is the common good which motivates their creation. As previously explored, radical social enterprises are radical because they do not support the existing capitalist status quo and actively attempt to create a different system based on common goods and internal goods being higher in the hierarchical ordering of goods. In MacIntyrean terms, radical social enterprises contribute to attempts to form local political communities through encouraging community members to participate and decide on the common goods of the community. Radical social enterprises can also provide the lead by example in attempts by others to contribute to the common good and would be deemed politically radical where they foster other, similar institutions in the locale. In a MacIntyrean sense, they are also radical in that participants within radical social enterprise promote the idea of a wider and locally political, common good. Similar to MacIntyre's example of the fishing community, radical social enterprise can be identified as organised by community members who appreciate that their individual interests are only served through the achievement of common goods in the process of operating the radical social enterprise for a social purpose. Participants in a radical social enterprise understand, then, that they are part of a deliberate alternative to the existing economic order in which capitalism and the pursuit of profit are dominant. They actively seek alternative paths to the mainstream order of capitalism to demonstrate an alternative economic model which prioritises the social purpose above financial gains. Kay et al. identify an alternative conceptual framework for radical social enterprise which shifts the focus from economic impact of an activity to social and environmental impacts. They argue that the framework creates a fairer method of exchanging goods and services through realising economic activities are not an end in themselves, rather a means to an end. They further identify three ends to which radical social enterprises can have an impact; social, environmental and societal, creating an enhanced role for radical social enterprise in which it is recognised that their activities impact on the relationships between individuals and communities. The framework's shift in focus from economic priorities can be likened to MacIntyre's view that economic activity should be directed towards achieving common goods, which was explored in the common goods themes of this chapter and in Chapter 2. Kay et al. suggest that social enterprises, and particularly radical social enterprises, should ensure they have a positive impact on wellbeing and prosperity. They argue that radical social enterprises have a responsibility towards society and its culture to ensure that their impact is positive on the people and groups it interacts with. Furthermore, radical social enterprises play an important role in changing cultural and societal norms away from an economic focus towards the common good (Kay et al., 2016). Similarly, MacIntyre argues for the social conditions necessary for human flourishing to subordinate external goods such as economic gains, to common goods and internal goods. The implications of the conceptual framework are that social enterprises will recognise that adding to the economy is not an end in itself, instead it can create opportunities for 'good work' in accordance with Pearce (2003). Furthermore, not having to economically contribute, creates a broader understanding of contribution in society which can include voluntary labour, shared ownership of goods and alternative ways of exchanging goods and services.

Again, consistent with the above understanding of radical social enterprises, MacIntyre (2016) considers the different approaches to efficiency and growth in his comparison of the fishing crews highlighting that it is an issue of the ends being pursued. The cooperative fishing crew demonstrate a commitment to the ends of sustaining their community over economic ends of profit. As explored previously, he argues that to do so they demonstrated the virtues of prudence, justice, temperateness and courage which are necessary for a community to flourish (MacIntyre, 2016). More specifically, prudence requires good judgement in political and economic matters, particularly when operating in a dominant capitalist market. Notably, radical social enterprises are also required to practice prudence (as understood by MacIntyre) in their decisions and actions so that they can maintain their focus on their social purpose and not succumb to the external goods associated with the capitalist enterprise and individual self-interest which capitalism encourages (MacIntyre,

2007). Reflecting this MacIntyrean virtue they must instead entrench their social purpose and commitment to alternative market methods in their structure and through their everyday actions and decisions to withstand the pressures of a capitalist society which values the individual over the community (MacIntyre, 2007). Moreover, the creation of a radical social enterprise is specifically for the purpose of addressing injustice in society and their operating methods also therefore demonstrate a commitment to justice (again as understood by MacIntyre). Radical social enterprises also demonstrate temperateness in their activities (again as understood by MacIntyre) through limiting the share of profits to ensure the social purpose is prioritised and wages which are not excessive. It is important therefore to note that the people who work at Coexist accept only a 'living wage' in favour of developing the common good of the community and creating an alternative organisational form, not based on economic wealth (Larner, 2014). Lastly, courage (again as understood by MacIntyre) is necessary for radical social enterprises to ensure they maintain their commitment to the common good, whilst operating in a dominant capitalist system. They must ensure they resist the temptations from the private sector towards becoming more 'business-like' and focusing on profits, or towards a reformist social enterprise, playing a supporting role to the state and business (Pearce, 2003). Kay et al. (2016) point out that despite capitalism being to blame for many of the social injustices, they suggest that it is widely believed that capitalism with a social element could be the remedy. However, it has been discussed in Chapter 5 how corporate social responsibility is flawed in terms of the common good and maintains a focus on individualism and external goods. Capitalism, even with corporate social responsibility, is not a suitable approach to resolving the injustices associated with it because they will prioritise external goods before common goods. Members of radical social enterprises, therefore, need courage to withstand the dominance of attitudes in society which see capitalism as the only option but which run counter to the common good. They also need courage to resist the temptation to make trade-offs between internal and external goods so compromising the hierarchy of goods according to MacIntyre. Consistent with this analysis, Kay et al. argue that their alternative conceptual framework can redefine the relationships between individuals and groups, which will influence and change the cultural norms in society towards a culture that promotes the common good. As we have also seen, Pearce too identifies the shared values in social enterprise as cooperation, collaboration, inclusiveness and democratic decision-making, which, it has been argued here, can be applied to the conceptual framework to define how radical social enterprises aim to influence and generate positive impacts on community and society. It is in this context that we can also use MacIntyre's understanding to make better sense of radical social enterprise practices, as he argues that a concern for the common goods of society is necessarily political because to engage and deliberate on such issues we must *also* engage politically with others in any given society.

MacIntyre (2016) describes the elements necessary to the politics of making and sustaining local communities and the common good, as shared deliberation, agreement on the goods at stake, a shared conception of how goods should be achieved, with every relevant voice being heard and given due weight, outside the influence of the arbitrary exercise of power or influence. It is argued here that radical social enterprises contribute to these MacIntyrean processes, through their efforts to create local communities and the common good through their social purpose and the democratic ways in which they operate politically. For example, Larner describes Coexist as having a cooperative approach in which democratic decision-making, is central to the process of ensuring that common goods remain the focus of the organisation. More specifically, the structure of radical social enterprises, particularly in the context of the above alternative conceptual framework supplied by Kay et al., ensures that economic considerations are not the ends being pursued but rather, the means to achieving the social outcome desired. In other words, the power and influence in radical social enterprises are not based on capital ownership; decisions are instead based on a shared understanding of what is in the interests of the local community, based on the further democratic assumption that those affected by the decisions have a right to their voice being heard. Participants in radical social enterprises agree on their social purpose because this is established when it is created. Nevertheless, *how* the social purpose will be achieved is subject to ongoing decisions and activities which are subject to the democratic decision-making which involves shared deliberation by all those affected. Similarly, MacIntyre (1999) argues that a society which nurtures the relationships of giving and receiving, which are necessary for individual and common goods to be achieved, must have shared deliberation, justice and political structures which enable all voices to be represented in accordance with what he calls, 'just generosity'. He further argues that intermediate structures between state and family are needed to create networks of giving and receiving which meet the requirements of just generosity, recognising that our ability to participate in decision-making and shared deliberation can change at different points throughout our lives (MacIntyre, 1999). It is argued here that radical social enterprises directly reflect MacIntyre's view of giving and receiving through their shared deliberation in determining their activities towards their social purpose; a commitment to justice demonstrated through their social purpose and rejection of the capitalist status quo; a focus on the common good in their purpose; and an understanding of acknowledged dependence demonstrated through their social purpose in a community.

For MacIntyre, then, a community of networks of giving and receiving (which can now include radical social enterprises as understood here) do not encourage economic growth in favour of social considerations. Thus, individualism, acquisitiveness, profits and wealth as ends in themselves must be replaced by a concern for the common good through shared deliberation and action. Consistent with this understanding, radical social enterprises, it is argued here, promote a social purpose in a community and reject capitalism and the economic priorities associated with it, in favour of using economic resources only as a means to achieve their social ends, which are determined collectively. It is also argued here that participants in radical social enterprises, when engaged in promoting this purpose, are understanding common goods as existing prior to individual goods (consistent with MacIntyre). In the process, radical social enterprises also promote the virtues of shared deliberation and just generosity and (again consistent with MacIntyre) thereby choose to be antagonistic towards the existing capitalist order (MacIntyre, 2016).

Radical Social Enterprises as Institutions

According to MacIntyre (2007), institutions provide the external goods to support their practices and because of external goods being money, power and status, these practices are vulnerable to institutions becoming too acquisitive. Institutions, therefore, need virtues to ensure their practices remain their focus and do not succumb to institutional potential to pursue external goods (MacIntyre, 2007). Chapter 2 elaborated on MacIntyre's view that capitalist institutions focus on external goods to the detriment of practices, and, subsequently, internal and common goods. MacIntyre claims, too, that modern society has a focus on individualism which encourages people to act only to serve their own interests. MacIntyre instead argues that to achieve their own goods, people must first consider the goods they have in common with their community, both locally and more broadly. MacIntyre considers that the virtues and the ability of the practice maintain integrity are largely determined by the institution which supports the practice. The type of institution is, therefore, critically important to the pursuit of practices and the achievement of individual and common goods. MacIntyre identifies cooperatives as the type of enterprise which support practices which achieve common goods. It is argued here that radical social enterprises can also be considered as institutions which support practices which achieve common goods, whilst also rejecting the capitalist market system and actively creating viable alternatives. To effect any real change to the dominance of the capitalist system, it is necessary to create viable alternatives which will encourage people to realise that there are alternatives to capitalism. It has already been argued in Chapter 6 that capitalism promotes itself as the only viable option for society, and therefore, it is important to demonstrate working alternatives. Radical social enterprise represents such an alternative because it rejects the capitalist model of fixating on external goods, in favour of common goods. As explored in this chapter, the foundation of a radical social enterprise is a social purpose which is aimed at improving the common good of a community, as in the example of the Community Kitchen at Coexist; it is run for the benefit of the community to encourage and teach cookery skills, provide food for those in need and a place for companionship and support. Therefore, we might say that radical social enterprise has a social need as their primary goal and external goods are used as a means to achieve that end as reflected in a strict hierarchy of ordering of internal goods over external goods, in order to promote the primary common good. Moreover, the radical social enterprise as an institution (and understood in MacIntyre's terms) is structured to ensure that decisions are taken through shared deliberation by all affected and not based on capital ownership and founded on shared values which form the basis for how the organisation operates. However, as previously highlighted, Pearce (2003) acknowledges that there is a lack of philosophical underpinning to its values and purpose. It is argued here, and throughout this book, that MacIntyre can provide such a philosophical underpinning which recognises radical social enterprise as an institution supporting practices and the common good in communities and, in turn, contributing to the flourishing of these communities.

It is also argued here that we must acknowledge the need to engage in debates such that we achieve a better understanding of the precise relationship between values and goods. The distinction made between hierarchical ordering and trade-offs of internal and external goods, with the strict ordering of internal over external goods, leads to a radicalised understanding of social enterprises that can more sharply distinguish these institutions from reformist social enterprises and socially minded traditional businesses. The argument is that reformist social enterprises and socially minded traditional businesses, while not relying on promoting a maximising profit as the only value (characterising neoliberal capitalism), nevertheless rely on a much more compromised trade-off between internal and external goods. This argument in turn has been found to better reflect and articulate MacIntyre's views on capitalism which would clearly support the radical social enterprise as defended by Pearce in this book.

Developing this application of MacIntyre to Pearce's position the chapter will now examine how Pearce elaborates a vision of social enterprises via the fictional example of Anytown, in which a group of residents take action against the problems associated with industrial decline, recession and high unemployment in their community. The group hold community meetings to identify key problems and possible strategies for tackling them and to agree future activities (Pearce, 2003). The first decision being to create a community enterprise called Anytown Community Enterprise (ACE) with the aim of finding an alternative approach to private and public sector methods (Pearce, 2003). In this fictional town, ACE aids new ventures to establish themselves and gradually new social enterprises develop in the town to encompass a range of services including childcare, recycling services, housing, job creation and training, particularly for those disadvantaged in the employment market. Pearce suggests this process as being based on 'subsidiarity' through the town council relinquishing control of services to the community enterprises helped and promoted by ACE. The various social enterprises in the town are run with a mixture of paid and volunteer labour, enabling the efficient use of resources and creating opportunities for non-financial reward; the town also operates a barter system in which people can trade skills and goods (Pearce, 2003). All of the social enterprises in Anytown are community owned and seek to improve the quality of life in the locality (Pearce, 2003). All the social enterprises created as a result of ACE have a social purpose at their core, not the accumulation of individual wealth.

This purpose is achieved through cooperative ownership and democratic management of the organisations, which develop and encourage volunteer labour, barter and exchange and paid labour. ACE is viewed as the catalyst for growth of social enterprises in the town.[1] In short, Pearce's Anytown is an example of how social enterprises can promote the common good through institutions which are committed to their social purpose and not to the external goods of wealth and prestige. However, Pearce also argues that radical change is needed to move away from the dominance of capitalist markets, towards replacing it with this kind of Anytown model. He also identifies the mutual approach with the cooperative movement in which people organise themselves through mutual and self-help methods. He cites Robert Owen in arguing that common interests must be prioritised over individual interest to ensure a social system which benefits all. Radical social enterprise, therefore, represents both the mutual model that Pearce propounds and his belief that an alternative to the dominance of capitalism is needed. Whilst MacIntyre suggests that cooperatives represent an institution which supports the common good, radical social enterprises are also common good-supporting institutions whilst also rejecting capitalism in their organisation.

So, how does this model and Anytown fit with MacIntyre, and how can the latter be used to articulate more fully the values promoted via the practices of the former? Radical social enterprises engage in economic activity only for purposes of achieving their social purpose and in doing so encourage networks of giving and receiving in which their social objectives can be achieved. Their success is measured in terms of their social impact, rather than economic profit, so the promotion of income and wealth is reserved solely for the social purpose of sustaining the organisation for it to continue achieving its social aims. MacIntyre (2016) argues that 'contribution' in capitalist societies is largely measured in economic and monetary terms, whereas it should be measured in terms of the common good. Radical social enterprises are founded on their

[1] Although Pearce is describing a fictional town, there has been a significant growth in social enterprises since the work was written in 2003. There are now social enterprise towns and cities, notable of which is Alston Moor in Cumbria which was awarded the status of the first Social Enterprise Town in 2012 by Social Enterprise UK, the national body for the social enterprise sector in the UK. The town is made up of villages and hamlets and has social enterprises providing shops, broadband, transport and various other services to the community. In an area which was suffering from industrial decline, social enterprises have enabled the community to respond to its own needs.

social purpose and, therefore, contribute to the common good with the implication that individuals within the enterprise also contribute to the common good by their role within the organisation. Furthermore, it has been argued previously that individuals participating in a radical social enterprise, implicitly or explicitly, understand their role in relation to the common good, which would have motivated them to become involved with the organisation in the first place. MacIntyre, as was also argued, points out that individuals who are concerned about common goods and work towards addressing them, are acting politically. The politics of local community require a democratic approach to decisions and actions, enabling shared deliberation and democratic decision-making. The radical social enterprise members engage in shared deliberation, but which extends beyond the enterprise to the wider community and a democratic decision-making process which is not based on individual power or ownership. Developing these arguments here, then, we might also say that the institutional structure encourages discussion and active participation in how common goods can be achieved. Radical social enterprises are generally small-scale based in local communities and address local needs. This is consistent with MacIntyre who also argues that the small-scale character of local communities is better able to share common goods and emphasising that the virtues of just generosity and shared deliberation are essential for the community to flourish. It is also argued here that radical social enterprises use shared deliberation to determine how to meet their social objectives through their activities and can also demonstrate the exercise of MacIntyrean virtues. That is, just generosity through actions that create justice for those who need it through the promotion of social purpose; generous and beneficent actions through voluntary work and the commitment and dedication by the participants to the common good; and also a sense of pity for others who are worse-off which motivates those involved to act for the benefit of the social purpose. Moreover, it is the contention here that it is via these virtues (as understood by MacIntyre) that we can explain why radical social enterprises are involved in, for example, homelessness, mental health, disability related access to work and numerous areas which are aimed at improving the lives of people in communities and their common good. According to MacIntyre (2016), cooperatives demonstrate the virtues in their commitment to the common good and similarly, according to the arguments defended here, radical social enterprises operate cooperatively to ensure that common goods are achieved through shared deliberation. They also operate democratically to ensure that all relevant views are considered, without the influence of profits and wealth being determining factors in the decision-making process. Radical social enterprises are community-based institutions which encourage participation by local people in the development of common goods. This is achieved through an organisational model which does not prioritise profits and wealth but uses it as a means to achieve the social purpose for which it was established. MacIntyre's philosophical view of how virtues and common goods are developed can, therefore, be used to articulate the values associated with social enterprise, giving them a solid foundation instead of the vague terminology that Pearce identified with the general appeal made by radical social enterprises to promoting shared values. In MacIntyrean terms, then, those participating in radical social enterprises are committed to creating institutions which encourage practices and common goods. Thus, a radical social enterprise is a democratic, cooperative institution which works to develop the common good in a community, through shared deliberation and a shared understanding of the goals at stake. In so doing, the participants develop practices which work towards these common goods. That is with external goods associated with economic profit-making and wealth creation being used merely as a means to achieve common goods, and the promotion of internal goods specific to the social goals defined and promoted by the radical social enterprises. Finally, participation in the radical social enterprise enables individuals to appreciate the role of common goods and deliberate on how they can be best achieved, together with their simultaneous promotion of commensurate individual goods.

Conclusion

The aim in this book has been to identify elements of MacIntyre's work with Pearce's social enterprise, with the intention of creating a philosophical underpinning for social enterprise. Whilst Pearce's vision of social enterprise provides an outline of the purpose and practices of social enterprise, it is the elaboration of his radical form of social enterprise which provides the most fertile ground for fully synthesising MacIntyre's theory, because it includes a rejection of capitalism and the individualism and capital wealth accumulation associated with it. Pearce's social enterprise characteristics and values and MacIntyre's practices and institutions theory have been synergised to create a framework for radical social enterprise. The characteristics and values which Pearce identifies indicate an affinity to MacIntyre through a social purpose which has priority over external goods. Indeed, social enterprises protect their assets and wealth so that it can continue with the social purpose. They are structured to ensure that shared deliberation and democratic decision-making include all members of the community and encourage participation in what MacIntyre would describe as a politics of making and sustaining local community. This book has identified as significant in both MacIntyre's and Pearce's work the themes of common goods, rejection of capitalism, cooperation and democracy, which have been discussed in greater detail to reveal the compatibility of MacIntyre's thoughts on virtues and institutions with radical social enterprise. The rejection of capitalism is fundamental to the radical social enterprise because they are created as an alternative form of organisation to capitalism, with a specific aim of demonstrating a viable alternative in which profit and wealth creation are used solely for the purpose of contributing to the common good based on a shared social purpose. Radical social enterprises are, therefore, distinct from reformist social enterprise as defined in Chapter 6, with the latter tending to operate in areas where the state has withdrawn support such as social services and there are insufficient profits to encourage capitalist enterprises to invest. Subsequently, it has been argued here, reformist social enterprises work in conjunction with the state *and* capitalism to support areas of society which have been neglected by these systems, as discussed earlier in this chapter and in Chapters 5 and 6. Whereas radical social enterprises are attempting a more political role according to Pearce (2003) which more fundamentally challenges the dominance of capitalism. The difference between radical and reformist social enterprise is significant because, as Pearce argues, it is not possible to collaborate with the capitalist system, whilst introducing an alternative. Similarly, MacIntyre argues that the economic focus of capitalism must be rejected if society is to create the political and social structures which support the common good. It has been explored how both MacIntyre and Pearce recognise that economic ends associated with capitalism and individualism are inimical to the collective behaviour necessary to achieve the common good. The radical social enterprise approach identified by Pearce is also described by Kay et al. (2016) in a conceptual framework which clearly depicts the social enterprise as measuring its social impacts and using economic activity merely as a means to do so. Furthermore, the framework identifies the societal impact of the social enterprise in terms of its influence on both individuals and groups, with the purpose of contributing to a culture which promotes the common good. The framework, therefore, creates a political role for social enterprise in terms of changing societal and cultural norms through their activities and operating methods. This is also significant in relation to MacIntyre's work because it represents a viable organisational form which is committed to the common good, whilst also rejecting capitalism. In MacIntyrean terms then, radical social enterprises are helping to create flourishing communities which do not measure success in economic terms, but in terms of wellbeing and human flourishing. There is though capitalist resistance to organisations which operate in this way; both MacIntyre and Pearce acknowledge the difficulties associated with operating outside of the capitalist system. Pearce acknowledges the temptation for radical social enterprises to become more 'business-like' in their activities or become more reformist in their approach and consequently engage in trade-off behaviour contrary to the hierarchical approach advocated by MacIntyre and Pearce. MacIntyre (2016) argues that efficiency and growth are measured differently depending on the ends which are to be achieved. He further argues that the virtues are necessary for the ends to be understood as flourishing communities, rather than serving the end of economic efficiency. Similarly, radical social enterprises are dedicated to the common good and use alternative forms of growth which are not measured in economic terms and can, therefore, demonstrate the virtues of prudence, courage and justice, when they are successful in contributing to the common good in a sustained way. Moreover, radical social enterprises have a democratic approach to decision-making that involves all those affected by their activities, which is also akin to MacIntyre's view on creating flourishing communities. Members of radical social enterprises contribute to their local community by engaging in activities which promote the common good and, moreover, share an understanding of how it can be achieved. Decisions are, therefore, based on the needs of the community as conceptualised by that community, rather than an economic gain. Furthermore, radical social enterprises encourage similar organisations to adopt their approach, which can enable wider cooperation between organisations and a stronger defence against the dominance of capitalism. Pearce points out that such organisations promote and publicise their alternative approach when describing the radical form of social enterprise. Thus, it is argued here, that radical social enterprises can be viewed as institutions which support the common good and develop the virtues in the individuals who are involved in the organisation's goals. The primacy of common goods over individual goods creates an environment which cultivates giving and receiving with just generosity which again reflects MacIntyre's position. Radical social enterprises act in a manner which demonstrates an alternative to capitalism and contribute to attempts to form local political communities through their activities and promoting values which encourage wider participation. They, therefore, represent a democratic, cooperative approach in which ownership is not based on capital contribution, which is again consistent with MacIntyre's views on the type of organisation which promote the common good. Moreover, it is argued here that radical social enterprises are a clearer and less ambiguous representation of MacIntyre's view of a common good supporting institution compared with a more general promotion of cooperative organisations as propagated by MacIntyre. In short, radical social enterprises are more consistent with an outright rejection of capitalism which is necessary to create the kind of radical change promoted by both Pearce and MacIntyre. Finally, it is in this latter context too, that a more specific understanding of shared values can be understood and promoted (so addressing Pearce's concerns about the ambiguity and vagueness about what these values might mean), again, as demonstrated here, using MacIntyre to articulate these values more clearly.

References

Ballard, B. (2000). *Understanding MacIntyre*. University Press of America.

Centre for the Understanding of Sustainable Prosperity. www.cusp.ac.uk (Accessed 17 May 2019).

Defourny, J., Hulgard, L., & Pestoff, V. (2014). *Social enterprise and the third sector: Changing*. Routledge.

Jackson, T. (2017). *Prosperity without growth: Foundations for the economy of tomorrow* (2nd ed.). Routledge.

Kay, A., Roy, M. J., & Donaldson, C. (2016). Re-imagining social enterprise. *Social Enterprise Journal, 12*(2), 217–234.

Knight, K. (1998). *The MacIntyre reader*. Polity Press.

Larner, W. (2014). The limits of post-politics: Rethinking radical social enterprise. In J. Wilson & E. Swyngedouw (Eds.), *The post-political and its discontents: Spaces of depoliticisation, spectres of radical politics*. Edinburgh University Press. *European landscapes in a comparative perspective*. Routledge.

MacIntyre, A. (1999). *Dependent rational animals: Why human beings need the virtues*. Carus Publishing Company.

MacIntyre, A. (2007). *After virtue* (3rd ed.). University of Notre Dame Press.

MacIntyre, A. (2016). *Ethics in the conflicts of modernity: An essay on desire, practical reasoning and narrative*. Cambridge University Press.
Pearce, J. (2003). *Social enterprise in Anytown*. Calouste Gulbenkian.

CHAPTER 8

Conclusion

My aim in this book has been to consider whether social enterprise can represent an institution which develops the virtues through internal goods and common goods, consistent with MacIntyre's philosophical work. A thorough understanding and analysis of MacIntyre's work on practices, virtues and institutions has been essential to this process. Furthermore, his antipathy towards capitalism has been elaborated to demonstrate the role of radical social enterprise as a viable alternative to capitalism, which, it has been argued here, is a form of institution that develops the virtues through a focus on common goods. Despite MacIntyre's views on business and capitalism, there have been numerous attempts to align his work on virtues with business activities. Most notably, Moore (2005b, 2015) has written extensively on the possibilities for business to be virtuous and has created a set of virtuous characteristics for businesses to be deemed as virtuous. As a result, it has been necessary to explore the validity of the efforts to align business with MacIntyre's work. However, it has been contended throughout this book that capitalist business cannot be virtuous because they are focused on profits and wealth, rather than on practices and the associated internal and common goods. MacIntyre advocates for a hierarchy of goods in which external goods are strictly subordinate to common goods and internal goods. Moore (2005b) developed a model of virtuous business in which businesses, if they behaved in accordance with his model, could be deemed virtuous. However, Moore

G. Hall, *Virtue and Social Enterprise*,
https://doi.org/10.1007/978-3-031-14027-3_8

tends towards describing business as needing to balance goods, which is contrary to MacIntyre's view that there can be no balance, only a strict ordering of goods in which external goods such as wealth are subordinated. However, there are institutions which could be practice embodying and do not use a balance between goods, indeed, MacIntyre (2016) cites cooperatives as examples in his work. Thus, institutions which are categorised as different to capitalist business were analysed to determine their affiliation with MacIntyre's views. Social enterprise as a trading organisation which has a social purpose represented significant possibilities in being aligned with MacIntyre's institutional role of supporting practices. A thorough analysis of social enterprise, its characteristics and its role in the economy and society was therefore necessary to determine its congruence in relation to MacIntyre. There was found to be a broad consensus on the basic characteristics of a social enterprise, but significant differences of opinion with regard to where social enterprise fits within the economy. Chapter 5 explored the spectrum theory of social enterprise in which they could be categorised as ranging from corporate social responsibility carried out by capitalist business, through to charitable foundations with a trading aspect to their endeavours. However, I have argued that the spectrum theory fails to acknowledge the fundamentally different origins of social enterprise and capitalism. Furthermore, it fails to acknowledge the strict hierarchy of ordering goods in accordance with MacIntyre. Capitalism, it has been argued, carries out philanthropic activities, determined by the owners and controllers of capital, in order to redress the inequalities and injustices occurring from the capitalist mode of conducting business. Whereas social enterprise was born out of the social and cooperative movements in industrial Europe, established by individuals and communities to address social ills. Pearce (2003) developed a theory which clearly separated social enterprise from capitalist and private business and created a model which identified three systems within the economy, of which social enterprise was part of the third system in which social purpose was key. Capitalist and private business formed the market driven element as the first system, in which private gain and profit orientation were the focus. Pearce's analysis of the values and characteristics of a social enterprise were detailed to establish their relationship with MacIntyre's work in Chapter 7. Pearce (2003) identified that the values associated with social enterprise tended to be rather vague. To redress this issue, the values and characteristics were aligned with MacIntyre's work, particularly in relation to practice, goods, democracy, cooperation and politics. Particular attention was paid to Pearce's distinction between reformist and radical social enterprise, whereby the former collaborates with the existing capitalist system and the latter seeks to replace it. It has been made clear in the exploration of MacIntyre's views that he rejects capitalism and the individualist, consumer driven society it creates. Thus, radical social enterprise represented the most appropriate form of institution to align with McIntyre, whilst also being a viable alternative to capitalism that is already in existence. In Chapter 7 analysis of MacIntyre's work on virtue together with the radical form of social enterprise was carried out. This analysis demonstrated a compatibility between them which has implications for the breadth of application of MacIntyre's theory and creates a philosophical basis for radical social enterprise values.

Essential to investigating the compatibility of MacIntyre's work with radical social enterprise was a thorough understanding of MacIntyre's work on virtues. For MacIntyre (2007), practices are important in the attainment of virtues, it is through a sustained commitment to a practice that individuals develop the virtues and central to that development is a focus on individual and common goods. MacIntyre distinguishes between internal and external goods, demonstrating the importance of focusing on internal goods for the achievement of virtues. Crucial to understanding MacIntyre's work is to appreciate the importance of common goods in his approach to virtues and the hierarchy of goods. He determines that common goods of family, workplace and community should be the focus, before we are able to determine our individual goods. Without such prior understanding of the goods we have in common, it is not possible to fully conceive of our own goods. He views the virtues of just generosity and acknowledged dependence as central to the appreciation of common goods. The appreciation of our connection to others in family, workplace and community and our mutual dependence is what enables us to determine the goods that we have in common. MacIntyre argues that such awareness and actions to address common goods are political actions in making and sustaining local communities. Institutions are central to MacIntyre's approach as they house the practices which develop the virtues. However, MacIntyre (2007) argues that the institution must focus on the internal goods of the practice, rather than external goods if virtues are to be achieved. The institution would need to develop the virtue of acknowledged dependence and create networks of giving and receiving in which shared deliberation could determine the common goods to be pursued. MacIntyre asserts cooperation as a key feature in the pursuit of virtues and refers to cooperatives and community organisations as examples of institutions that demonstrate such characteristics. However, MacIntyre is scathing of the current economic order in which capitalism dominates within a free market that encourages individualism and an erosion of community and common goods. Despite MacIntyre's views of capitalism, various scholars have attempted to align his view of a virtue embodying institution with business organisations. Indeed, Moore has written extensively on how businesses could be virtuous if they could demonstrate commitment to a set of virtuous characteristics that he has created. However, Moore acknowledges that capitalism would need to be changed in order for his characteristics to gain traction. I have contended throughout this book that capitalism is not compatible with MacIntyre's work because it demands that external goods are the priority which is quite at odds with a hierarchy which places external goods as subordinate to internal goods. The focus on wealth creation for the owners and managers of capital preclude the pursuit of practices in a MacIntyrean sense. The purpose of the organisation impacts on the ability to focus on practices and the excellence necessary for development in the practice. Indeed, Beadle (2008) argues that capitalism creates an inversion of priorities whereby external goods become the focus. Furthermore, he suggests that MacIntyre makes no distinction between capitalism and enterprises and therefore, they are all equally incompatible with his views. Capitalism encourages external goods through effectiveness which is at the expense of the practice and the pursuit of excellence in that practice. I have argued that capitalism is driven by capital formation which involves employing the surpluses created by the workforce into further wealth creation and not for the benefit of individuals trying to pursue practices. Thus, where organisations focus on the external goods of wealth and prestige, rather than the internal goods associated with practices as, it is contended here, is the case with capitalist business, there can be no alignment with MacIntyre. However, there are organisations which play an economic role that could be compatible with MacIntyre. Beadle (2008) argues that a fuller interpretation of MacIntyre to include the importance of common goods, power balance and political economy in his work is essential to ensuring that an institution can embody the virtues. MacIntyre is clear that external goods are still goods but should not be allowed to overpower internal goods in the priorities of the institution. To fully interpret MacIntyre is to realise that common goods are prior to individual goods and to accept that individual goods cannot be achieved without first understanding this. When individuals do appreciate their common goods and take, what MacIntyre would deem as political actions towards the pursuit of common goods in the form of an institution that enables shared deliberation in determining those common goods, then it becomes a reflection of MacIntyre's views. Critical for MacIntyre is the power balance in an institution which allows for deliberation by all individuals, without bias or influence. Hence, his reliance on cooperatives as examples of practice embodying institutions. My contention has been that social enterprises could represent a practice embodying institution in accordance with MacIntyre. Social enterprises are institutions which have a social purpose which is achieved through some form of trading. There is broad agreement on the characteristics of a social enterprise across Europe whereby they have a social purpose, limit their distribution of profit, engage in trade and encourage wide participation in their decision-making and governance. However, there is disagreement by academics on the positioning of social enterprise within the wider economy with views ranging from them being part of capitalist business through philanthropy and corporate social responsibility, to being the trading branch within the charitable part of the economy. The view held in this book is consistent with Pearce's theory that social enterprises are not part of the capitalist, private enterprise system within the economy, which prioritises personal gain and profits. Instead, they form part of the social system of the economy in which social purpose and mutual support are the mainstays. The alignment of social enterprise with capitalist philanthropy fails to recognise its historical antecedents in the social movements, such as the Cooperative movement, resulting from the Industrial Revolution in which capitalists pursued wealth at the expense of labour. Such movements had their origins in self-help, mutual support and democratic participation, rather than the wealth creation of capitalist organisations. Pearce (2003) acknowledges the history and the predecessors of social enterprise and reflects them in his analysis of the characteristics and values which identify this type of organisation. Social enterprises according to Pearce, operate through the characteristics detailed above and are founded on the values of cooperation, decentralisation, inclusivity, good work, sustainability and people-centred. It is the characteristics and values which formed the basis of the analysis with MacIntyre's work in Chapter 7. Furthermore, Pearce recognised the political role of social enterprise in encouraging members of communities to participate in developing its common goods. He identified two forms of social enterprise as reformist and radical in which the former supports and collaborates with capitalist business, whilst the latter is trying to create an alternative to capitalism. Given its commitment to being an alternative to capitalism and the political role in encouraging individuals to pursue their common goods, it is my view that radical social enterprise represented the most appropriate form of enterprise to consider in the context of MacIntyre. Indeed, I have argued that capitalism increases the wealth and power of the owners of capital to the detriment of the workforce and the majority of society. Kay et al. (2016) identify that there is increasing realisation that free-market principles do not serve society, particularly since the global financial crisis of 2008. Radical social enterprise has the potential to become the alternative to capitalism which serves society, rather than the minority of owners of capital. I have argued that capitalism is founded on private ownership, individualism and profit orientation; whereas social enterprises are founded on common interests, shared ownership and a common good orientation. It is therefore argued that the current dominance of capitalism serves the interests of the owners of capital who accumulate wealth through profit-oriented organisations. The capitalist system encourages individualism at the expense of common interests according to MacIntyre to further the pursuit of wealth by the owners of capital and production. Thus, capitalism serves the owners of wealth through institutions which focus on efficient and effective methods of creating profits. Whereas, social enterprises are created by cooperative actions by community members to address a common interest. They operate through democratic decision-making based on shared interests, rather than capital investment and have aims which are orientated to common goods.

The analysis throughout this book identified the significant elements of MacIntyre's work and the key factors in the structure and development of social enterprise. Furthermore, a broader understanding of both MacIntyre and Pearce identified the significance of rejecting capitalism in a virtue embodying institution. The key elements of social enterprise were synthesised with MacIntyre's work in Chapter 7. It was determined that all of Pearce's characteristics and values of social purpose, engaging in trade, non-profit distribution, common ownership, accountability, cooperation, decentralisation, inclusivity, good work, sustainability and people-centred could be aligned with MacIntyre. In particular, the politics of making and sustaining communities and common goods to create flourishing communities according to MacIntyre was reflected in Pearce's radical social enterprise. MacIntyre has argued that institutions focus on the internal goods of their practice to ensure that individuals achieve their internal goods and contribute to common goods. To do so, external goods need to be secondary to internal goods. Radical social enterprises ensure a focus on internal goods and common goods through their primary purpose being social rather than financial as in the case of profit-maximising businesses. They are therefore akin to MacIntyre in the hierarchical ordering of goods to ensure that external goods such as wealth are not dominant. The radical social enterprise as an institution is established for achieving a common good for a community and prioritises that good above capital concerns such as shareholders. It has been argued that in radical social enterprises there is a reversal of focus in relation to capital and labour in which labour employs capital to achieve its social ends, unlike capitalist institutions where capital employs labour. The social purpose of the radical social enterprise was identified with MacIntyre's common goods because they are established for the purposes of achieving an improvement in social value in some aspect of a community, as in the case of the Community Kitchen at Coexist. Furthermore, the cooperative structure and common ownership of radical social enterprises align with MacIntyre in relation to his views on the virtues being developed through practices in cooperative structures such as Thorupstrand and Monte Azul. Radical social enterprises engage in forms of trading but retain the social purpose as the primary focus and limit profit distribution to ensure this. Similar to MacIntyre, Pearce views radical social enterprise as having a political role in increasing democratic involvement of people in communities to create decentralised local politics, with an inclusive approach in which decisions on local issues and common goods are determined at local level. In MacIntyrean terms, they are engaging in local politics of making and sustaining communities. Pearce describes good work as a value in social enterprise by which he means work that is socially useful and enhances quality of life in general or for a specific group. Further, he identifies being people-centred as a key value whereby the enterprise serves the interests of people, not profits or wealth. The application of MacIntyre's virtue work gives Pearce's terms of 'good work' and 'people-centred' a distinct focus and meaning which is lacking in the rather vague terminology. Both good work and people-centred can be aligned with the purpose of a practice to develop the virtues through a sustained effort to develop excellence in a practice, which ultimately benefits the community through common goods, as well as the individual through internal goods. MacIntyre's focus is the flourishing or wellbeing of communities through common goods being deliberated and developed and virtues are achieved through a commitment to practices and excellence. Radical social enterprises demonstrate such a commitment to practices through a focus on the social purpose and limited external goods such as wealth for the owners of capital. Despite the values of social enterprise being described as vague by Pearce, it can also be argued that the value of sustainability in which the environment is linked to the activities of the social enterprise can give a broader scope to MacIntyre's work. MacIntyre does not make specific reference to sustainability or the environment, although it can be implied in his focus on flourishing through virtues. However, radical social enterprise in the context of capitalism and the depletion of natural resources present a viable alternative which does not subscribe to the view that capital accumulation at the expense of the environment is acceptable. The radical social enterprise model is based on sustainability for both the institution and for wider society in not creating harmful environmental impacts or exploitation of natural resources in the pursuit of wealth. Aligning MacIntyre's work with radical social enterprise creates a philosophical underpinning for an existing model of enterprise activity which can be fully implemented as a viable replacement for capitalism.

The development of MacIntyre's work with radical social enterprise identified parallels between them, which were developed into common themes, with the overarching understanding that both MacIntyre and radical social enterprise subscribe to the hierarchical ordering of goods. Namely: rejection of capitalism, common goods, cooperation and democracy. The rejection of capitalism is crucial to MacIntyre's conception of virtues because capitalism creates and encourages the individualism and acquisitiveness which are antithetical to the pursuit of the virtues. Similarly, radical social enterprises are viewed by Pearce as a radical alternative to capitalism in which the social purpose and regard for communities and society are paramount. MacIntyre refers to cooperatives as embodying an institution that focuses on practice; radical social enterprises represent a broader interpretation of the type of institution which can encourage the virtues through their social purpose and commitment to common goods. They can be identified as creating networks of giving and receiving in accordance with MacIntyre through their focus on a social purpose, whilst pursuing measures of success such as social impact, rather than traditional capitalist business which is measured in financial terms. Capital is used in radical social enterprise for the furtherance of social objectives, unlike capitalist business in which the aim is to extract as much surplus value as possible from labour for the accumulation of wealth. Furthermore, radical social enterprises can be aligned with MacIntyre, with both advocating a strict hierarchical ordering of goods in which external goods are subordinate to internal goods. Radical social enterprise, unlike capitalist business is dedicated to the achievement of social outcomes which benefit a particular group or community, rather than wealth and prestige. Thus, they develop common goods which are determined through shared deliberation, which leads to a distinction between internal and external goods to shared practices so that the latter is intentionally subordinated to the former. Whereas, socially responsible businesses cannot cohere consistently with MacIntyre's or radical social enterprises strict hierarchy of goods because they are more susceptible to engaging in a trade-off between internal and external goods.

The social purpose of radical social enterprise can be assimilated with common goods in accordance with MacIntyre because the social purpose is developed from the needs of a community. They are established by individuals who collaborate to create a social impact where a need arises, as in the example of Coexist (Larner, 2014). In accordance with MacIntyre, those individuals are concerned with the common goods of their community and take what MacIntyre would deem a political role in trying to sustain and develop their community. MacIntyre cites acknowledged dependence as a virtue, which can be demonstrated in radical social enterprise through the commitment to ensuring that individuals get support to achieve their individual goods as well as common goods through the social purpose. An example used in Chapter 6 of a café which supports people with dementia clearly demonstrates an understanding of the need to support people who are no longer able to fully achieve their own goods. MacIntyre and Pearce both cite cooperation as crucial in their work because it provides for decisions on how to achieve the social purpose or common goods to best be determined, through equal and unbiased discussion that is without capital influence. MacIntyre (2016) would describe such communications as shared deliberation to achieve common goods. It has been argued here that radical social enterprise as a form of cooperative represents a more appropriate example of MacIntyre's views because of the explicit rejection of capitalism. Indeed, Pearce suggested that social enterprise can trace its roots back to medieval guilds and social movements that stressed the importance of cooperation towards a common social purpose. Essential to the cooperative approach in radical social enterprise is the democratic decision-making process to ensure that social purpose is the focus and to contribute to local democracy through participation by community members in its decisions and actions. Similarly, MacIntyre views those who engage in pursuing common goods are taking a political role in creating and sustaining local community. Indeed, he argues that a political society in which communities engage with their common goods is essential to developing the virtues. It has been argued that radical social enterprises encourage engagement with common goods and as such contribute to attempts to form local political communities and encourage others to do so.

Radical social enterprise has been shown to represent a MacIntyrean institution in which common goods are achieved through practices and a commitment to finding an alternative to capitalism. Furthermore, they can be viewed as radical in a MacIntyrean sense because they promote the idea of a locally political common good through encouraging participation in local political communities in which common goods can be determined. Radical social enterprises demonstrate an alternative economic model in which social purpose is prioritised over financial gains. Or in MacIntyrean terms, they subordinate external goods to internal goods in pursuit of a common good. Moreover, there is a shift in focus in which economic activities are subordinated to the social goals of the organisation and only serve as a means to achieving those goals. Kay et al. (2016) identified three ends to be pursued in radical social enterprise as social, environmental and societal and argued that they play an important role in changing cultural and societal norms towards an appreciation for the common good, rather than the economic focus dominant in capitalist economies. They also identify that such an approach creates a fairer method of exchanging goods and services because economic gain is not the primary focus (Kay et al., 2016). The change in focus which removes the demand to contribute economically creates a much broader understanding of what it means to contribute in the workplace, community and society. Such contributions can include voluntary labour and alternative methods of exchanging goods and services which enables greater numbers of people to contribute to the common goods in their community. This combined with a MacIntyrean interpretation of 'good work' in which practices are the means to achieving internal goods and common goods provides an expansive role for radical social enterprise in contributing to a change in society in which the capitalist focus on individualism and economic gain is no longer paramount. Kay et al. (2016) have argued that social enterprise can create well-being and prosperity in society, which is not linked to economics, allowing for an understanding of what creates value beyond economic prosperity and consumerism. MacIntyre's interpretation of the place of virtues in creating wellbeing and flourishing can be applied to the behaviour and outcomes of radical social enterprise to create a working example of an organisational type which could encourage them.

Afterword

The social economy has evolved since the financial crisis of 2008 (Roy, 2021). There are a number of contributory reasons for the evolution, most recently the COVID pandemic in 2020 has created a focus on community and shared endeavour towards a common end of preserving life in the face of the pandemic. Such common cause has found expression within the social economy because it was always aimed at the care and wellbeing of society. In the UK, austerity measures to counteract the financial crisis of 2008 have also increased the need for support to those in society who are less able to thrive in a market driven environment. Furthermore, there has been an ever-increasing realisation and recognition of the harm being caused by climate change and environmental degradation, which has also been reflected in the social economy organisations established to protest and counteract such harms. Child (2021) argues that despite the economic and social issues brought to the fore by the pandemic, there has been a renewed sense of community through people working together to overcome the challenges presented by COVID-19. Furthermore, in the context of climate change, Child emphasises the need to develop a participatory approach in society in order to overcome the challenges. However, there remains an emphasis on the individual in cultures and societies dominated by free-market capitalism. Indeed, Monbiot (2021) asserts that corporate marketing strategies have contributed to a change from collectivist action to individual. He describes it as a political change which has converted people from being citizens to consumers. Monbiot points out that as consumers we are considerably less powerful than as citizens; where people view themselves as citizens, they can act collectively to bring about political change. In ecological terms, this has translated into a focus on individual contribution to climate change, such as recycling at home and plastic bag usage. Meanwhile, the greater crisis being created and exacerbated by large-scale corporations is considered beyond our power to change (Monbiot, 2021).

According to *No Going Back: State of Social Enterprise Survey 2021*, social enterprises have shown resilience and growth during the COVID-19 pandemic (SEUK, 2021a). The report identifies a 44% increase in turnover, compared to an 18% increase in mainstream business. Further, the report argues that social enterprises show greater sustainability, even during economic crises such as the pandemic and should become the mainstay for our economy and society (socialenterprise.org). Indeed, the Organisation for Economic Cooperation and Development (OECD) suggests that the social economy has the potential to create systemic change in society, towards a more sustainable economy. They argue that organisations within the social economy are well placed to influence policies and decisions to aid recovery in the wake of the COVID-19 crisis. The OECD contends that COVID-19 has shone a light on the failings in society when faced with a global pandemic. They suggest that the social economy has shown an alternative approach which makes best use of community and people empowerment, when faced with a crisis. Indeed, they point out that the crisis has increased the creation and visibility of social economy initiatives which now have the opportunity to play a bigger role in creating a more sustainable and inclusive society (www.oecd.org). Social Enterprise UK (SEUK) in a follow up report, *One Year On: The Effect of COVID-19 on the Social Enterprise Sector*, in April 2021 identified that a large number of social enterprises had increased and adapted their activities during the pandemic. This was in response to the needs of the community, with changes in activities focused on wellbeing in terms of mental health and access to services. The report also identified an increased interest in community and a related growth in social enterprise creation (www.socialenterprise.org). Similar to the OECD, the report also emphasises the opportunity for social enterprises to demonstrate their ability to meet social and community needs, whilst identifying as different to mainstream capitalist business. The Chief Executive of SEUK, Peter Holbrook sees the pandemic as an opportunity to learn from the weaknesses of the current dominant system and create an economy which focuses on social inequalities and the environment. The report hopes the pandemic crisis will engender a renewed appreciation for cooperation and mutuality (SEUK, 2021b).

Laville (2014) views the social economy as organisations with a variety of ownership, in contrast to the capitalist economy in which ownership rests with investors. The enterprises within the social economy are owned by various stakeholders such as workers or the community, in which profits or accumulation of capital is not the priority. Laville (2014) suggests these types of organisations develop reciprocity through social connections, rather than individual interest. It is worth pointing out that MacIntyre's acknowledged dependence can be viewed similarly to the reciprocity created by such organisations in which giving and receiving in equal terms are understood as central to the role of the enterprise. In other words, organisations within a community would support those in need whilst recognising that everyone may need such support, regardless of their position in society, that we are all indeed, equal in terms of our need for good health and wellbeing.

The wellbeing economy essentially requires us to reconsider what we value and therefore how we measure growth in an economy. The neoliberal approach to the economy is to create economic growth on the basis that such growth will benefit all. However, there is plenty of evidence to suggest that such policies only benefit the wealthy. The disparity in wealth is clearly evidenced in the statistics cited by Vatn (2020) in which the richest 20% of the population receive 83% of income globally, whilst the poorest 20% receive 1%. It is argued that economic growth has not benefited society fairly, the wealth that has been created has benefited the wealthy few, to the detriment of the environment and the majority of people (Fioramonti, 2017). Indeed, there are increasing calls to question what to measure in society and the economy and to rethink what makes these things successful (Fioramonti, 2017; Roy, 2021; Wellbeing Economy Alliance, 2022). In particular, the fundamental problem with capitalism in a market economy is the inability to focus on anything other than economic growth and accumulation of material wealth. Even where there are efforts to mitigate damage caused by capitalism, such as corporate social responsibility activities, I would argue the underlying reason for this behaviour is to protect the wealth and future business prospects of the organisation. Jackson (2021) points out that growth in society is not the problem, but rather that capitalist growth is the issue because profit is the driving force for investors. Profits as the primary motivation for investors in capitalism have created the drive for economic growth that has led to ecological and social instability (Jackson, 2021). In a capitalist system, growth is based on Gross Domestic Product (GDP) which relies on increasing incomes to reflect growth. Thus, prosperity is measured in economic terms. Through such a measure, the non-monetary aspects of society are not counted in terms of prosperity. Furthermore, capitalism cannot or will not provide a solution to its own shortcomings because it is not in the interests of the investors to do so (Jackson, 2021). I concur with Jackson that it is essential that alternatives to economic growth are developed and move towards an understanding of prosperity which is sustainable for both society and the environment.

Prosperity without growth forms the title and subject for Jackson's (2017) research and gives a clear understanding of prosperity understood in much broader terms than economic growth. Indeed, it could be argued that prosperity has very little to do with money and more to do with human flourishing and wellbeing. This type of prosperity would have a greater focus on society and how we live together on a planet with finite resources, rather than how much wealth we can accumulate. Social progress would be measured in terms of a reduction in human impact on the environment and living well, without consuming more than is sustainable (Jackson, 2017). Jackson refers to balance being key to prosperity rather than growth, referring to Aristotelian virtues being the mean between extremes. Similarly, MacIntyre (2007) also refers to the Aristotelian balance between extremes when considering virtues. Indeed, Aristotelian virtues provide helpful instruction when considering the issues with capitalism and its pervasive influence on society, which is considered within this book. Essentially virtue explores character, rather than behaviour in that it is our moral character which determines our behaviour. MacIntyre (2016) believes that questions about growth are both moral and political and suggests that the primary concern should be about the ends to be achieved. Inherent to this are the virtues; it is only through virtues such as prudence, courage, justice and temperateness that discussions about growth can have a meaningful impact on the common good and sustainable wellbeing. MacIntyre (2016) refers to examples of communities which have thwarted the influence of capitalist markets to develop sustainable and flourishing communities. However, he also points out that where such endeavours founder or are threatened by the free market capitalists, the mainstream economic thought assumes it is because these communities and organisations are inefficient and hinder growth. He cites the virtues as being essential, for example, the virtue of temperateness is essential for ensuring the lure of capitalist wealth is resisted. MacIntyre argues that modernity, through capitalism has altered the correct understanding of virtues derived and lived throughout an entire life. This has been replaced by what he refers to as pleonexia, which in Aristotelian terms is greed for material wealth. Clearly, pleonexia is endemic in capitalism because of the profit motive, which creates a continuing desire to acquire goods and services. MacIntyre (2015) argues growth in capitalist, economic terms as being for the benefit of the owners of capital. Pleonexia or acquisitiveness in relation to economic growth involves continual acquisition and growth, beyond a basic level of need and security. Clearly, there is still a need for the acquisition of basic living needs and security in developing countries, whereas in Western countries, for the most part, do not require a continued economic growth to provide such essentials. Particularly given the threat to the earth being created by our over consumption, it has become a matter of urgency that we review economic growth as a measure in society and politics. We should reconsider the value of continued acquisition of material possessions, given the increasingly evident impact on society and the environment. MacIntyre (2015) points out that growth only occurs in an economy because capitalists are able to benefit from profits, which are in turn, the results of labour contribution to goods and services. According to MacIntyre, capitalism is obliged to portray itself as the means to ongoing economic growth, which must be viewed as positive, in order that society will continue to consume the goods and services which provide the capitalist profits. However, MacIntyre also points out that capitalism will ensure that costs pertaining to growth will be incurred by the worst off in society. This can manifest in a multitude of ways from homes being repossessed to deforestation harming both human and non-human habitats. MacIntyre asserts that virtues have become divorced from their original meaning because of the modern focus on individualism and a loss of shared community. A revival in the true understanding of virtue in which a balance between extremes and a greater awareness of viewing our lives in their entirety, rather than immediate self-interest, would have a positive impact on the way we live our lives. Furthermore, a greater understanding and participation in shared community which includes the natural environment will contribute to wellbeing and flourishing. The Aristotelian view of virtue is such that one person's good is bound to others' good. In other words, we are not simply individuals pursing our own interests, potentially at the expense of others, but rather, we rely on others to pursue our own goods. It is not possible to achieve our own flourishing in the true sense, at the expense of community. The common good is prior to individual good and therefore must be attended to first, in order to fully achieve our own good. This view of society would have a transformative effect on how we live and how we treat nature and the environment. If we understand that our own prosperity is intrinsically linked to others, both human and animal, then we may behave more humanely towards each other. Cooperation and collaboration towards greater wellbeing and sustainability for the natural environment are already the focus for some radical social enterprises. If this model were developed more widely, it would encourage a change in cultural understanding of how society can work. Kay et al. (2016) refer to such an alternative conceptual framework in relation to social enterprises, in which economic activities are the means to achieving their social outcomes. Rather than seeing social enterprises as businesses with a social agenda, they would be distinct in that their values identify an alternative way of doing things. They imagine that social enterprises could change the prevailing attitudes in our culture and society from competitiveness to cooperation. Furthermore, they argue that their paradigm for social enterprise would encourage a shift from the perpetual growth model to a broader understanding of how prosperity can be achieved.

Capitalism does not encourage the development or achievement of the common good, it is focused only on profit and wealth for investors; the owners of capital. If organisations such as radical social enterprise represent an alternative way of doing business, it is also necessary to consider the political aspects of their role in society. Wright (2012) believes that to change capitalism it would be necessary to create a more meaningful democracy through altering the power dynamic within the economy. It is acknowledged that capitalism has created the productive capacity to improve the lives of those living in economically developed countries (Wright, 2012). However, there is an ever-growing concern regarding the perpetual growth in production on a finite planet (Jackson, 2017, 2021). Furthermore, capitalism creates significant differences in people's ability to access those products and services that improve lives (Wright, 2012). MacIntyre (1999) also argues that equality is of critical importance to ensuring a political community achieves the common good. Vast differences in wealth create an unequal society which is perpetuated by the strength of the interests of the wealthy. Thus, in order to create a society where business considers their values before profits, there must be consideration for where democratic power lies. MacIntyre (1999) also argues for the rejection of capitalism and economic growth, which are inimical to an economy which promotes the common good.

Roy (2021) suggests that social enterprise research needs to embrace the wider issues of politics and democracy to fully realise the potential for social enterprises to influence government and the economy. MacIntyre (2016) refers to examples of communities which have demonstrated a commitment to the common good and refers to their politics. He argues that it is necessary to engage with the state and the market to bring about a change in a political activity.

The Wellbeing Economy Alliance (WEALL) has a vision in which society will transition from the narrow focus on economic growth measured through GDP, to alternative measures which encompass the wellbeing economy. GDP measures the level of national income in monetary terms based on all products and services a country produces. However, there has been criticism since its inception after the Second World War and the Great Depression (WEALL, 2020). Prominent figures such as Robert F. Kennedy in 1968 identified that GDP fell far short of measuring any worthwhile elements in life. Nevertheless, the influence of GDP is all pervasive, with most people at all levels of a society understanding that it affects them in some way. It is generally assumed that growth in GDP is positive and creates prosperity, and a decline is negative and could result in job losses and detrimentally affect society. However, there are alternative ways of measuring the progress of a society which go beyond only wealth and take into consideration factors such as environmental degradation and wellbeing. According to Constanza et al. (2018), there is a global movement towards changing from measuring economic growth, to a greater focus on sustainable wellbeing. The Scottish Government assesses its performance through a National Performance Framework which takes into consideration social and environmental progress as well as economic; the framework measures national wellbeing (Scottish Government). Scotland alongside Iceland, New Zealand, Wales and Finland form the international governmental approach to altering the focus away from economic growth to a more balanced emphasis on wellbeing (Wellbeing Economy Governments initiative WEGo). A wellbeing economy considers both human wellbeing as well as nature and the environment. Implicit is the understanding that society and nature are interdependent and therefore a holistic approach is needed to achieve prosperity (Costanza et al., 2018). It is worthwhile to note here that there are considerable numbers globally of individuals and organisations which aim to achieve such a change in societies. The Wellbeing Economy Alliance (WEALL) was created to unify all the diverse approaches to a wellbeing economy and create a global movement towards changing the hegemony of economic growth. Roy (2021) likens the Aristotelian view of flourishing with wellbeing when considering the meaning of living a fulfilled and 'good' life. Furthermore, Roy suggests that the economy should be considered in much broader terms to encompass the state and community. If we recall Pearce's Three Systems of the Economy, all elements of society are represented from family through to the state. It is clear from the diagram that there are a multitude of ways in which people contribute to society, aside from the dominant free-market view of economic contribution. Many in society are unable for various reasons, to make an economic contribution but nevertheless, contribute in other ways. The wellbeing economy would take into consideration such contributions and value them accordingly.

To achieve a wellbeing economy, one of the fundamental issues is to alter the focus on profits for the owners of wealth, to a society which values prosperity in a holistic sense, rather than being driven by wealth creation. Inherent to this aim are the organisations such as radical social enterprises which seek to create alternative sources of prosperity, without the need to maximise profits. Coscieme et al. (2019) identify that a wellbeing economy will require businesses to be driven by their purpose and have social and environmental aims. I would argue that radical social enterprises are an example of such organisations. However, the focus on economic growth also ignores the multitude of non-economic activity that occurs in society. Pearce (2003) identifies the third system of the economy as including all the activities such as child-care, family support, schools and churches which are essential to running a society, yet do not provide an economic output which can be measured in GDP terms. It is through the multitude of communications and support which go unrecognised in economic growth which form the heart of society and what should be measured. It is in the links made at this micro level of political society that radical social enterprises serve to mobilise and support members of communities towards their own and others' wellbeing.

Roy (2021) considers social enterprises as organisations that aim to improve wellbeing and which could contribute to the development of a 'wellbeing economy'. In harmony with the Scottish Government's National Performance Framework, it is the first country to develop a social enterprise strategy to support achieving the objectives of wellbeing and sustainable growth (Scottish Government, 2016). Roy (2021) suggests a dearth of research into the relationship between social enterprise and wellbeing and what is available is relatively recent. Nevertheless, he cites a growing range of research into the role social enterprises play in addressing both individual and community health and wellbeing factors. Roy and Hackett (2017) identify that social enterprises could contribute to changes in the political economy, suggesting that local initiatives could contribute to meaningful changes in society towards wellbeing. Roy (2021) notes a methodological concern in relation to wellbeing research in which there can be a focus on the individual, which is then aggregated to reflect an impact on a community or population as a whole. This, Roy points out is a challenge because societies are not simply a sum of individuals. I believe that MacIntyre's views on community represent a solution to this challenge as he tells us that the common good is prior to individual good. Indeed, in MacIntyrean terms, there is no individual good before the common good is determined in as much as, individual goods are derived from the common good (Murphy, 2003). In terms of wellbeing, the common goods of a community can be identified with all the elements Roy identified as pertaining to wellbeing, such as health and education. Blake (2019) has applied MacIntyre's views in research into the contribution social enterprises make to wellbeing. Blake views social enterprises as practice-based institutions in accordance with MacIntyre and sets out to determine whether or not practices within social enterprise contribute to individual wellbeing, albeit in a small-scale study. She argues that engagement in practices and the achievement of excellence can contribute to wellbeing for the practitioners in accordance with MacIntyre. Whilst I agree with this argument, I would suggest that MacIntyrean virtues also have a more conceptual benefit to bring to the academic research into social enterprise and wellbeing because they contribute to the common good and therefore, wellbeing in society as well as individual wellbeing. Thus, I would argue that the virtues demonstrated in radical social enterprise, detailed in Chapter 6, represent a theoretical demonstration of the contribution they can make to the alternative economies needed for the future.

MacIntyre, Alternative Economies, Radical Social Enterprise and the Social Economy

Pearce (2003) pointed out that in his three systems of the economy that the third system represents an alternative approach to the private enterprise of the first system. He asserts that there are common values which underpin this system which are quite distinct from the other systems. The values which Pearce identifies include cooperation, decentralisation, inclusivity, good work, sustainability and people-centred. Furthermore, Pearce views the third system as representing an alternative to challenge the first system. He argues the constitutive elements of the social economy have values which include democratic decision-making, a focus on the common good for both humans and the environment and local economy, sustainable working practices and prioritising people before profits. Additionally, the social economy is viewed as the platform to develop civil society and encourage democratic participation (Defourny, 2001; Edwards, 2009; Martin & Thompson, 2010; Pearce, 2003). I have already identified that Pearce viewed radical social enterprise as an alternative approach to the political and social economy. I would argue that radical social enterprise represents one of many approaches which are being developed towards creating alternative economies which reflect the needs of society and the environment. Furthermore, I believe that MacIntyre's work can be linked to this. I have discussed MacIntyre on giving and receiving and would argue that his view of those unable to contribute to a community in terms of practical rationality could include the environment and non-human animals. MacIntyre argues that in a flourishing community, an important indicator is the individual flourishing of those unable to contribute due to age, infirmity etc. I would argue that this indicator of flourishing can be extended to include the environment and non-human animals. That is not to say that such elements do not make a contribution, as clearly, they do. For example, the environment, such as woodlands have an invaluable role to play in terms of wellbeing, air quality amongst many others. However, they are not able to participate in the practical reasoning required to organise a flourishing community in MacIntyrean terms. Extending from this point, the common good being prior to individual good would also include these considerations. MacIntyre (1999) points out that community goods are more than simply the sum of individual goods. Indeed, they are prior to and inform the individual's goods. Thus, the environment and non-human animals included in the common goods of a community become an essential element of that community's flourishing. In other words, if individuals aspire to a flourishing life in accord with the virtues, they understand that nature and the environment, both locally and globally, are essential to the common good.

References

Beadle, R. (2008). Why business cannot be a practice. *Analyse & Kritik, 1*, 1–13.

Blake, J. (2019). Utilising a MacIntyrean approach to understanding how social enterprise may contribute to wellbeing. *Social Enterprise Journal, 15*(4), 421–437.

Child, J. (2021). Organisational participation in post-covid society—Its contributions and enabling conditions. *International Review of Applied Economics., 35*(2), 117–146.

Constanza, R., Caniglia, B., Fioramonti, L., Kubiszewski, I., Lewis, H., Hunter Lovins, L., McGlade, J., Mortensen, L. F., Philipsen, D., Pickett, K. E., Vala Ragnarsdottir, K., Roberts, D., Sutton, P., Trebeck, K., Wallis, S., Ward, J., Weatherhead, M., & Wilkinson, R. (2018). *Towards a sustainable wellbeing economy.* http://www.researchgate.net

Coscieme, L., Sutton, P., Mortensen, L. F., Kubiszewski, I., Costanza, R., Trebeck, K., Pulselli, F. M., Giannetti, B. F., & Fioramonti, L. (2019). Overcoming the myths of mainstream economics to enable a new wellbeing economy. *Sustainability, 11*, 4374.

Defourny, J. (2001). Introduction: From third sector to social enterprise. In C. Borzaga & J. Defourny (Eds.), *The emergence of social enterprise.* Routledge.

Edwards, M. (2009). *Civil society* (2nd ed.). Polity Press.

Fioramonti, L. (2017). *Wellbeing economy: Success in a world without growth.* Macmillan

Jackson, T. (2017). *Prosperity without growth: Foundations for the economy of tomorrow* (2nd ed.). Routledge.

Jackson, T. (2021). *Post growth: Life after capitalism.* Polity Press.

Kay, A., Roy, M. J., & Donaldson, C. (2016). Re-imagining social enterprise. *Social Enterprise Journal, 12*(2), 217–234.

Larner, W. (2014). The limits of post-politics: Rethinking radical social enterprise. In J. Wilson & E. Swyngedouw (Eds.), *The post-political and its discontents: Spaces of depoliticisation, spectres of radical politics.* Edinburgh University Press

Laville, J. L. (2014). The social and solidarity economy: A theoretical and plural framework. In J. Defourny, L. Hulgard, & V. Pestoff (Eds.), *Social enterprise and the third sector: Changing European landscapes in a comparative perspective*. Routledge

MacIntyre, A. (1999). *Dependent rational animals: Why human beings need the virtues*. Carus Publishing Company.

MacIntyre, A. (2007). *After virtue* (3rd ed.). University of Notre Dame Press.

MacIntyre, A. (2015). The irrelevance of ethics. In A. Bielskis & K. Knight (Eds.), *Virtue and economy.* Routledge.

MacIntyre, A. (2016). *Ethics in the conflicts of modernity: An essay on desire, practical reasoning and narrative.* Cambridge University Press.

Martin, F., & Thompson, M. (2010). *Social enterprise: Developing sustainable businesses*. Palgrave Macmillan.
Monbiot, G. (2021, October). Capitalism is killing the planet—It's time to stop buying into our own destruction. *The Guardian*. https://www.theguardian.com/environment/2021/oct/30/capitalism-is-killing-the-planet-its-time-to-stop-buying-into-our-own-destruction (Accessed 9 December 21).
Moore, G. (2005b). Corporate character: Modern virtue ethics and the virtuous corporation. *Business Ethics Quarterly*, *5*(4), 659–685.
Moore, G. (2015). Corporate character corporate virtues. *Business Ethics: A European Review*, *24*, S99–S114. https://doi.org/10.1111/beer.12100
Murphy, M. C. (2003). *Alasdair MacIntyre*. Cambridge University Press.
Pearce, J. (2003). *Social enterprise in Anytown*. Calouste Gulbenkian.
Roy, M. J. (2021). *Towards a 'wellbeing economy': What can we learn from social enterprise?* http://www.researchgate.net
Roy, M. J., & Hackett, M. T. (2017). Polanyi's 'substantive approach' to the economy in action? Conceptualising social enterprise as a public health intervention. *Review of Social Economy*, *75*(2), 89–111.
Scottish Government. National Performance Framework. *What it is*. https://nationalperformance.gov.scot/what-it (Accessed 16 November 2021).
Scottish Government. Scotland's Social Enterprise Strategy 2016–2026. https://www.gov.scot/publications/scotlands-social-enterprise-strategy-2016-2026/ (Accessed 17 November 2021)
Social Enterprise UK. (2021a). *No going back: State of social enterprise survey 2021*. https://www.socialenterprise.org.uk/state-of-social-enterprise-reports/no-going-back-state-of-social-enterprise-survey-2021 (Accessed 13 October 2021).
Social Enterprise UK. (2021b). *One year on: The effect of COVID-19 on the social enterprise sector*. https://www.socialenterprise.org.uk/policy-and-research-reports/one-year-on-the-effect-of-covid-19-on-the-social-enterprise-sector/ (Accessed 27 September 2021).
Vatn, A. (2020). Institutions for sustainability—Towards an expanded research program for ecological economics. *Ecological Economics*, *168*, 106507.
Wellbeing Economy Alliance (WEALL). *About*. Wellbeing Economy Alliance. https://weall.org/about (Accessed 15 November 2021).
Wright, E. O. (2012). Transforming capitalism through real utopias. *American Sociological Review*, *78*, 1–25.

Index

G. Hall, *Virtue and Social Enterprise*,
https://doi.org/10.1007/978-3-031-14027-3

T

V

W

The manufacturer's authorised representative in the EU is Springer Nature Customer Service Centre GmbH, Europaplatz 3, 69115 Heidelberg, Germany. If you have any concerns regarding our products, please contact ProductSafety@springernature.com

Printed and bound by CPI Group (UK) Ltd, Croydon, CR0 4YY
30/09/2026
02225490-0002